THE
AMERICAN FARM
TRACTOR

A History of the Classic Tractor

Text and Photography by Randy Leffingwell

Motorbooks International

This book is dedicated to the memory of Dick Bauer

First published in 1991 by Motorbooks International Publishers & Wholesalers, P O Box 2, 729 Prospect Avenue, Osceola, WI 54020 USA

© Randy Leffingwell, 1991

Motorbooks International is a certified trademark, registered with the United States Patent Office

The information in this book is true and complete to the best of our knowledge. All recommendations are made without any guarantee on the part of the author or publisher, who also disclaim any liability incurred in connection with the use of this data or specific details

We recognize that some words, model names and designations, for example, mentioned herein are the property of the trademark holder. We use them for identification purposes only. This is not an official publication

Motorbooks International books are also available at discounts in bulk quantity for industrial or sales-promotional use. For details write to Special Sales Manager at the Publisher's address

Library of Congress Cataloging-in-Publication Data
Leffingwell, Randy.
   The American farm tractor / Randy Leffingwell.
     p. cm.
   Includes bibliographical references and index.
   ISBN 0-87938-532-4
    1. Farm tractors—United States—History.
  2. Farm tractors—United States—Pictorial works.
I. Title.
S711.L34 1991
631.3′72′0973—dc20   91–3056

On the front cover: The 1957 John Deere Model 720 High Crop towers over the southwestern Iowa landscape. This Model 720 is owned by Robert Pollock.

On the back cover: Three of the most famous American farm tractors of all time: the Ford 2N, Minneapolis-Moline U-DLX Comfortractor and the Best 110 hp steamer.

On the frontispiece: A 1938 Graham-Bradley general-purpose tractor, owned by Dale Gerken of Fort Dodge, Iowa.

On the title pages: The John Deere Model 720 High Crop beneath the blue Iowa skies.

Printed and bound in Hong Kong

Contents

The origin of the word "tractor" was originally credited to the Hart-Parr Co., in 1906 to replace the longer expression "gasoline traction engine," which W. H. Williams, the company's sales manager, who wrote the advertisements, considered too cumbersome. The word actually was coined previously and was used in 1890 in patent 425,600, issued on a tractor invented by George H. Edwards, of Chicago.

US Department of Agriculture, *Power to Produce* handbook, 1960

Acknowledgments

The tractors in this book belong to patient, generous and enthusiastic individuals, each of whom gave me exceptional access to their collections and their time.

I wish to thank Daniel Best, Woodland, CA; Harold Chilcote, New Richmond, IN; Glen Christoffersen, San Carlos, CA; Virgil Chritton, Pomona, CA; Dick Collison, Carroll, IA; Victor Duraj, Davis, CA; Rich Eckert, Prescott, AZ; Cliff Feldkemp, Kaukauna, WI; Palmer Fossum, Northfield, MN; Dale Gerken, Fort Dodge, IA; Jeff Gravert, Central City, NE; Clarke and Ann Hall, Mountain Home, AR; Rusty Heidrick, Woodland, CA; Joan Hollenitsch, Garden Grove, CA; Don Hunter, Upland, CA; Jim and John Jonas, Wahoo, NE; James L. Keenan, Omaha, NE; Bruce and Walter Keller, Kaukauna, WI; Pat Mackin, Prescott, AZ; Roger Mohr, Vail, IA; Bob and Raymond Pollock, Dennison, IA; Frank Presley, Gridley, CA; Bill Rohr, Compton, CA; Paul Rumely, New York, NY; Norbert Schwabenlander, St. John, WI; Gary Spitznogle, Wapello, IA; Wes Stoelk, Vail, IA; Marv Sturgeon, Santa Barbara, CA; and Daniel Zilm, Claremont, MN.

Several people were extremely generous with their knowledge, libraries, introductions and time: Bill Cox, Pomona, CA; Palmer Fossum, Northfield, MN; Fred Heidrick, Woodland, CA; Helen Hutchings, Thousand Oaks, CA; Don Hunter, Upland, CA; Lester Larsen at the University of Nebraska, Lincoln, Tractor Testing; Roger Mohr, Vail, IA; Robert N. Pripps, Rockford, IL; and historian C.H. Wendel, Atkins, IA. These people gave me insight and direction, and taught me the difference between what was significant and what was merely fun.

Bob Campbell, Rudy Dremely and Virgil White of the Antique Gas & Steam Engine Museum, Vista, CA, gave unhesitatingly of their time and ideas. It is from them that the direction of this book originated.

Thanks to Leslie Stegh, Archivist, and John Gerstner with Deere & Company; to Kathy Mans and Joyce Luster with Caterpillar Inc., and to Douglas Rupp, Chief Accountant, and Bill Powers with Deutz-Allis, for their help and rapid fire information.

Robin Kirby of Brantford, Ontario, is working on a history of the Cockshutt Farm Equipment Company, and generously gave me the fruits of his research.

My thanks to John Clinard, Ford Motor Company, for the Aerostar which hauled me and hundreds of pounds of equipment around the countryside.

I must thank Motorbooks International publisher Tim Parker and my editor and friend, Michael Dregni, for suggesting this book. The look in their eyes that day was almost as gleeful as the experiences enjoyed in doing this project.

I am again grateful to Larry Armstrong, Bob Chamberlin and Cindy Hively on the photo assignment desk of the *Los Angeles Times*, for juggling schedules on my behalf.

Josef Hashbarger at A&I Color Lab, Los Angeles, cared for my Kodachrome, reassuring me regularly during my weeks on the road.

Lastly, I am deeply grateful to Lorry Dunning, University of California, Davis, Agricultural Machinery Collection, for prodding me and guiding me through the pitfalls and encouraging me onward when I stumbled.

To all of you who primed cylinders, released compression, tugged flywheels and awoke long before dawn or patiently watched me shoot till after dark—or directed me to those who would—my sincere thanks.

Randy Leffingwell
Los Angeles

Chapter 1

The American Farm Tractor

*The mere possession of tools, gadgets, machines, packages,
things is not enough. Wisdom requires an understanding of
what the march of technology can do to people and for people.*
Ezra Taft Benson, US secretary of agriculture,
foreword to *The Yearbook of Agriculture*, 1960

The history of farm tractors in America is one of cycles repeated: droughts and crop failures giving way to booms and overproduction giving way to wars and recessions; lower horsepower and smaller tractors giving way to higher horsepower and larger machines.

The industry has behaved like a not-always-benevolent giant. Inhaling and exhaling, it has suffered occasional hiccups, occasional indigestion. Occasional illness has brought weight loss and recovery. The giant has even suffered occasional surgery; in extreme cases, diseased limbs have been amputated and hearts have been transplanted.

This chronicle follows the development of the gasoline engine tractors, which were based on the preceding forty years of steam-tractor technology. In those forty years, the power of steam engines increased twenty-fold, with the greatest surge in power coming during the ten years after gasoline had been introduced and even as diesel power was being investigated. Gas

tractors would offer similar power output but in a smaller, less-expensive and more-maneuverable form.

The first portable steam engines were mounted atop horse-drawn wagons for mobility. The earliest gasoline traction engines resembled the steamers, in many cases being assembled out of the same parts bins. One historian has suggested that the familiar shapes of steam engines were used because they no longer frightened horses, so the new machines with their different sound would not startle the farm's draft animals. It is as likely that the gas engines followed the steamers' designs simply because these were the designs available. The builders of these first gas tractors were engineers, not stylists. It took enough work just to get the machines running reliably without adding the complication of changing their looks. So the Froelichs, Hart-Parrs and Russells broke new ground with their engines. Their resemblance to the steamers was not coincidence, it was convenience.

A sign of the blossoming American tractor industry at the turn of the century. Left, the 1913 Hart-Parr Model 30–60 was affectionately nicknamed "Old Reliable" due to its role as the iron workhorse on many early farms.

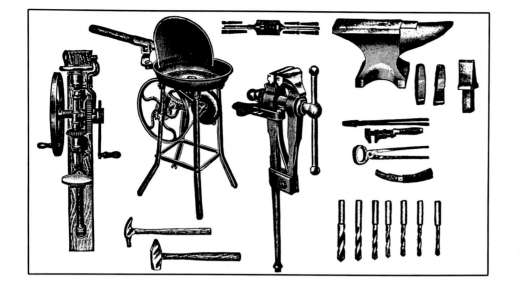

The recommended tools and blacksmithing equipment to care for an early gas farm tractor: drill press, smithing oven, vise, anvil, pliers and hammers. It is startling to think of how many tractor makers started with just these tools. Right, the H. W. Rice portable steam engine was typically fired by straw as wood was too scarce in central California where this engine was primarily used.

Tractors during the first fifteen years of gas power grew larger, as steamers had done. Their costs were substantial because research and development expenses had to be paid and because—from the days of the first mechanical reapers—the makers accepted time payments and charged interest in advance. Only the largest farm operators could afford the machinery, and they wanted equipment large enough to work huge spreads. In 1910, although there were 1,005,000 farms smaller than 20 acres there were 201,000 larger than 500 acres.

Demonstrations showed off tractor power, first at Winnipeg in Manitoba, Canada, then around the United States. But many early buyers discovered their expensive, powerful tractors were valuable only for initial prairie sod-breaking. The giants needed several people aboard them, just as the earlier steamers had, so they could handle fourteen plow bottoms. But they couldn't do the daily work as they couldn't maneuver between the rows to cultivate. Even small tractors converted from Model T Fords were not totally satisfactory. Horses were still needed.

The First World War needed horses too, and people by the millions. The US Army claimed "motor trucks" were still too unreliable to haul materiel or pull artillery, so horses and mules were drafted. The mortality rate was high. The farmers back home had no choice but to adopt tractors. But what they wanted were smaller, one-person tractors.

Some makers responded. Roughly fifteen years after John Froelich's first gas tractor, the Little Bull, Wallis Cub, Samson Sieve Grip, Fordson and Moline Universal redefined what the tractor could be and could do. America went tractor crazy, and nearly every inventor and almost every con artist got involved. Some tractor efforts were legitimate, and builders sold stock to go into business to produce their tractors. But some builders were simply in business to sell stock. If they ever produced a tractor, it was ill-conceived, inadequately tested and unusable. Fortunately for American farmers, one such machine was sold to a Nebraska legislator.

Wilmot F. Crozier purchased a Minneapolis Ford Model B and barely got it back to his farm before it broke down. It never worked as advertised, and he parked it in a corner of his field. Crozier then bought a secondhand Rumely Oil-Pull, which far exceeded its claims. He began to wonder how many other unreliable machines were out there and how he could force the makers to be more honest.

With the help of L. W. Chase, former head of agricultural engineering at the University of Nebraska, Crozier authored a bill he presented to the Nebraska House in 1919. By midyear, it was law, and companies with nothing to fear applauded it nearly as loudly as did the farmers. To sell a tractor in Nebraska, a firm had to have a sample tested in various prescribed ways. The first tractor tested was a Waterloo Boy Model N 12-25 hp, in April 1920. The tractor tests brought the desired result. Some builders who couldn't pass never came back; others made repairs and tried again. The Waterloo Boy passed the first time.

By then, the best tractors were produced either by men who were tinkerers or men who had grown up on the farm and knew from practical experience what was needed. Henry Ford was both. Ford tested models for years, then introduced his Fordson, so called because the firm that victimized Crozier also got to Ford: it registered the Ford trademark first.

The impact of Ford's tractor far surpassed its pulling power or its size. By adopting mass-production techniques to tractor assembly, as he had with his famous Model T automobile, Ford was able to produce the machine for less than his competitors could. But this equation relied on high production levels to work. When production dropped, Ford's expensive labor force and extensive factories cost him money. He cut his price so drastically that this too eventually redefined the tractor and the business.

At the beginning of the 1920s, there were 186 companies producing tractors in the United States; by the beginning of the 1930s, there were thirty-seven. Between Ford's pricing and Nebraska's testing—and a sluggish economy—more than three quarters of the companies quit the business. Those that stayed outlasted Ford, who quit himself in 1928, beaten at his own price war by International Harvester Company.

The International Harvester Farmall and the John Deere Model D profited from Ford's force-fed innovations. Company owners listened to their engineers, who had been listening to their customers for years. Manufacturers introduced, at last, a tractor for the masses, for row crops, for general farming purposes.

By the mid-1920s, most of the improvements that would see farm tractors through to the 1950s were in place. Electricity was still a relatively young development, and making it portable, self-contained and capable of producing high-voltage surges was a challenge that caused many farmers to curse the magnetos. New high-tension magnetos were coupled with spark plugs, and wet-cell batteries replaced the dry cells; by 1918, Moline's gangly Universal offered farmers the ease of turning a key. Self-starters cranked over the engines.

It was a marvelous change for the farmer. The tractor transformed him from being the source of the power to being the director of the power.
Robert C. Williams, *Fordson, Farmall and Poppin' Johnny,* 1987

Dust was the primary killer of tractors. Even as late as the 1920s, some makers left final-drive gears and clutches exposed to the silty, choking air. Internal engine lubrication was accomplished by gravity drip. When makers sealed running gear and pressurized the lubrication systems, when filter tanks of oil, water or even gauze were introduced to clean the air coming into the engines, tractor lives lengthened immensely.

Early tractors carried more water for engine cooling than gasoline for a day's running. Early systems ran water down screens, cooling by evaporation. Airflow was induced by running the engine exhaust through the "radiator," circulated by plunger-type pumps.

Early machines like the Heider moved the entire engine along a friction plate to increase speed or reverse tractor direction. Speed was limited by drive-wheel diameter, and the entire works needed careful alignment to provide proper friction to drive but not drag on the engine.

Tractor power was rated from the earliest days by the pull of the drawbar, which was used for drawing plows through soil, and by the power generated off the pulley wheel, which was used for operating threshing machines and the like. It was always quoted with those two numbers in that order: Waterloo Boy's 12-25 hp, for example. The addition of power take-off—a drive shaft running out the rear of the tractor to drive implements towed behind it—did not create a new rating. But standardization of the shaft placement, diameter and running speed created a uniform interchangeability of machines and made the farm tractor even more flexible.

If the tractor doesn't fit in with your system of farming, try changing your system of farming.
Wheeler McMillan, *Power Farming,*
1921

One last major innovation was poised for introduction by the late 1920s. German engineer Rudolf Diesel's engines were perfected for vehicle uses. In 1931, Caterpillar introduced its adaptation of the diesel for farm tractor use in its Model 65. A small gasoline engine, whose exhaust warmed the diesel cylinders, aided in cranking the main engine.

The worldwide Depression hit particularly hard on the farm. In 1932, thousands of farmers worked all year to earn 3¢ per pound from their hogs and 10¢ per bushel for their corn and to learn that their total annual production would not pay their $10 per acre rent. Foreclosures were common and became violent. The Farm Holiday—a holiday by no stretch of the imagination—spoke up effectively in behalf of the hard-working and underpaid farmer. Farm auctions were attended by fewer buyers than by farmers with axe handles. Private detectives were beaten and bankruptcy judges tarred and feathered. Times were hard, and Midwest farm families lived on beans for weeks on end.

By the mid–1930s, the costs of doing business, the stresses of competition and the Great Depression of 1929 had eliminated another half of the tractor producers who had been in business a decade before. Of the remaining twenty, nine controlled virtually the entire market. In the same decade, the number of tractors on farms had more than doubled, from about 506,000 to nearly 1,175,000 in use.

Styling, streamlining, and industrial design dressed up the giants by the end of the 1930s. Tractor makers observed the auto makers, and the designers and engineers learned of outside independents like Henry Dreyfuss and Raymond Loewy, who had streamlined America. These influences were not only tin deep. Dreyfuss and Loewy stressed as well that their work simplified manufacturing and improved the farmer's safety when using the more stylish machines. Separate logo colors were introduced by each maker.

In 1939, Henry Ford returned to the business with a remarkable new device and a new name attached to the tractors. Irishman Harry Ferguson had invented the three-point hitch, which enlarged the tractor's ability to plow while reducing the tractor's weight. The patented Ferguson System was so significant that it was mimicked by every tractor maker for the next fifteen years until the patents expired. But Ford and Ferguson's famous Handshake Agreement broke its grip much sooner. The two feisty, former farmers at last could only agree to disagree. Lawyers took over from there. The Ford Tractor with the Ferguson System broke new ground on American farms and in the American courts. This great twentieth-century patent battle gave a shallow victory to the inventor but showed big business the need for competent legal representation at all times.

Before the Ford-Ferguson war in court, the Second World War refined tractor production in America. The need for steel and rubber removed thousands of tons of obsolete tractors and machinery from farms. The government published posters: "A one horse cultivator can be made into two 60mm mortars, an old tractor can yield 580 .30 calibre machine guns." Tractors that were only old but not yet "antique" were gobbled up by the War Production Board. Manufacture of farm equipment was reduced as much as one third while spare parts production was ordered increased by half. Quotas were established, and farmers who had excess "scrap"—but who also had a growing sense of the history

The threshing bee in full steam on a Moody County, South Dakota, farm in the early years of the new century. This steam engine was being powered by burning straw, although it could also run on wood or coal. At least eight men are at work in this photograph, alongside the steamer, thresher, two wagons and two teams of horses.

of the machines—had to fight off the war drive, which wanted it all.

By the time the war ended, the number of tractors on farms had doubled again since the mid-1930s. The US Department of Commerce recorded nearly 2,422,000 tractors and registered a decline from more than 16,683,000 to 11,950,000 horses and mules.

Although progressive farmers were fascinated by tractors, economic realities held them back. Horses needed feed twice a day, year-round, whether working or not, but they were paid for, and the land raising their food was apportioned from the total farm—generally one fifth of the total acreage, as a rule of thumb. Tractors required fuel and repairs. Both had to be paid for in town. Farmers couldn't purchase new tractors for one fifth of their land and could barely make enough off that additional acreage to cover the costs of the tractors. A vicious circle of financing was coming into view. Farming by horse was not yet mortally wounded.

In 1947, a Canadian equipment maker, Cockshutt, introduced the next step in power take-off development with a continuous-running independent power take-off. Before Cockshutt's innovation, the power take-off shaft stopped running when the tractor drive clutch was disengaged, stopping the implement as well. Cockshutt fitted a separate clutch for its power take-off, meaning work continued whether the tractor was crawling at ½ mph, running at 4 mph or standing dead still.

New developments flooded the early 1950s. New hitching systems sped up the attachment or exchange of implements. Multispeed transmissions and gear-reduction systems, some providing eighteen speeds, let tractors get maximum engine torque at the speed the farmer chose. Liquified propane gas (LPG) was introduced as an inexpensive alternative to high-octane gasoline. Power steering joined with power implement lift to give the farmer's arms and back a rest. Even tractor seats got much-needed attention.

John Deere, long the traditionalist, held on to its tried-and-true two-cylinder Johnny Poppers for decades and then threw itself into the 1960s with a New Generation of four- and six-cylinder engines and tractors. For many, the New Generation of Power marked the end of an era, a sad passing; for others, it marked the first time they'd ever considered buying a John Deere.

Four-wheel drive, produced with little success in the 1920s and 1930s, returned by the late 1950s. In the early 1960s, as American manufacturers spiraled up the horsepower competition again, four-wheel drive became the most efficient way to transmit more than 150 hp, 200 hp and even 250 hp to the ground.

In the late 1960s, tractor history turned back on itself. The American manufacturers had steadily increased power output to such an extent that once again, few small tractors were in their lines. But the Japanese and Germans had them. Where average farm sizes were much smaller than those in the United States, a strong need still existed for tractors larger than the garden variety but smaller than 25 hp. Deutz of West Germany entered the US market with an air-cooled diesel in 1966. Satoh, eventually part of Mitsubishi Agricultural Machinery Co., was among the first companies from Japan; it brought in a 22 hp four-cylinder gas tractor in 1969. Kubota introduced 20 hp and 24 hp two-cylinder diesels in the United States in 1970.

By 1972, US manufacturers each offered large articulated four-wheel-drive tractors. The first tractors did not articulate or flex in the middle. All the wheels steered in the usual way, but the body did not; fronts turned, or rears turned, or fronts and rears turned and crabbing was possible. With Minneapolis-Moline's 1969 A4T, the axles remained fixed but the body bent in the middle. An extremely complex kind of universal joint allowed the halves to twist as well, accommodating wild changes in terrain.

Dual wheels front and rear denoted the next major spurt in power. And specialty manufacturers like Steiger, Rite, Rome and Versatile offered tractors with turbocharged diesel engines of 800 ci and 900 ci producing 400 hp, 500 hp and even 600 hp. These weren't show tractors meant for television stunts; they were meant for work like pulling disc harrow gangs 60 ft. wide.

Caterpillar stretched the technology envelope with its rubber-tracked Challengers. Steel reinforcement held the tread together even when run on paved roads between fields. The 325 hp 31,000 lb. diesel boasted half the ground pressure of a comparable wheeled tractor. Like its competitors, it even came standard with a dozen floodlights.

The family farm, in trouble since the Second World War, was hit from all directions. American trade protectionism crippled overseas produce sales, further stockpiling already unwanted grain. Prices plummeted. Farmers again faced foreclosure. Farm families wondered how to cope; they had scrimped and saved for college educations for their children, most of whom were then attracted to the far-better-paying jobs in the cities. In 1976, to stave off a return of the Farm Holiday as a result of farm foreclosures, Minnesota passed the Family Farm Security Act. In 1940, twenty-five percent of the US population lived on the farm; by 1980, only five percent remained. In 1980, the US Federal Reserve Bank raised its prime lending rate to 21.5 percent to halt inflation. No one could afford it.

The tractor industrialized the farm and the successful farmer needed the same skills as a successful industrial manager . . . he was a businessman who grew commodities such as food and fiber.
Robert C. Williams, *Fordson, Farmall and Poppin' Johnny,* 1987

With no one at home to work the family farm, no one in the family interested in inheriting the family farm, and the farmer tired and hoping for retirement, the future looked bleak. Burdened with equipment and education debt, farmers sold out. Looking to diversify and searching for tax losses—and what farmer couldn't assure them of that—corporations bought farms. Foreign corporations with low-value American dollars acquired potentially

high-value American real estate. By 1980, foreign investment in US farmland exceeded $1 billion.

The diseased giants heaved and sighed. "Surgeons"—specialists in corporate medicine—were called in. Harry Ferguson, after his divorce from Ford, went looking for a new partner, and in 1953, Massey-Ferguson resulted. In 1969, Oliver, Cockshutt and Minneapolis-Moline came together under the umbrella of White Farm Equipment. In 1984, International Harvester merged with J. I. Case, which had been held by Tenneco since 1967. In 1985, Deutz of West Germany bought Allis-Chalmers. Caterpillar and Deere slipped through unattached but not unscathed. Ford acquired New Holland Implement also in 1985 but moved its entire tractor production to England in an effort to centralize and stay in the tractor business.

The hostile takeover days of the 1980s meant that companies with funds to develop new machinery or reduce costs spent that money instead fighting off the raiders.

The farmers knew that scenario: Pests arrive in the fields and are treated. It costs money. And everybody complains about the taste it leaves in their mouth.

This book profiles the seven surviving tractor conglomerates through 1960, after which most collectors believe tractors are too new. Separate examinations of these productive giants are followed by a quick look at the ones that got away, the orphans that never found foster parents.

Roger Mohr's 1976 Minneapolis-Moline A4T Plainsman makes its way up the road near Mohr's Vail, Iowa, farm. The White-Minneapolis-Moline Model A4T–1600 was among the first of the factory-manufactured articulated four-wheel-drive high-horsepower tractors, and set the direction for the next two decades. Mohr's Plainsman 504 ci six-cylinder runs on propane and produces 169 hp.

16

Chapter 2

John Deere

*The country is now flooded with attempts at practical small
tractors and the extremely wide desire of the farmers to buy
such a small tractor cannot be entirely overlooked.*
George Mixter, superintendent of manufacturing,
Deere & Co., 1915

John Deere was born in Rutland, Vermont, on February 7, 1804. When he died on May 17, 1886, his implement company was enormous and successful. He had likely only just heard of the tractor; it was only four years before his death that John Froelich homogenized all the existing technologies into a self-propelled gasoline-engine-powered tractor.

John Deere the founder was succeeded by his son, Charles Deere the expansionist. Charles took the company out of the age of the horse through the age of steam and up to the age of internal combustion. Charles looked to the far horizons when he imagined the future of farming. Getting the company there was his largest accomplishment. When he died in 1907, he was succeeded by his son-in-law, William Butterworth.

Butterworth the acquisitionist ran John Deere the founder's company until 1928. He directed expansion into the last areas missing from the Deere & Company line-up, and apprehensively approved the purchase of Froelich's legacy in 1918. The Waterloo Gasoline Traction Engine Company became a Deere product and Deere became a full-line company. Five years later, the full-line company introduced its own tractor, a John Deere from the ground up. The Johnny Popper was born.

John Deere tolerated a short stay at Middlebury College, near his hometown of Rutland in Vermont. He escaped to apprentice with a local blacksmith who taught him quality artisanship. He adopted the standards and quickly found journeywork.

Deere's polished iron implements became legend. He married in 1827 at age twenty-three. As his family grew, they moved around Vermont before surrendering to its hard economy. Another Vermont native had moved to Grand Detour, Illinois, a new town located on the Rock River roughly 100 miles west of Chicago. Word came back that work was available, and in November 1836, Deere made a hard journey west.

The story goes that Deere arrived in Grand Detour with $73.73 in his pocket, and from this sum grew the great Deere & Company. Whatever the truth, he quickly established a regular blacksmith trade. And his regular trade came to him with problems.

Twenty-three John Deere General Purpose tricycles were built but currently only two are known to exist. The GPs quickly became available as wide-tread models, the GP WT.

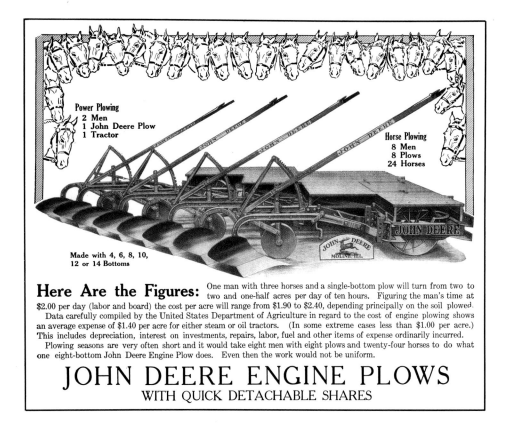

The plows that made John Deere famous, shown here in an ad from 1912. The formula for farming success was spelled out for all to see: power plowing was the way of the future versus the old-fashioned horse plowing. Right, the 1920 Waterloo Boy Model N was the first tractor tested by the University of Nebraska, from March 31 through April 8, 1920. Nearly 8,000 Waterloo Boys were sold between 1917 and 1924.

The soil around the Rock River was considerably stickier than that in Vermont. The dirt clumped so tightly to iron plows that constant scraping was required to continue. Deere, visiting at a friend's sawmill, spotted a broken steel saw blade, polished by thousands of cuts through coarse wood. Deere asked for the blade, and back at his shop, he cut off the teeth and fitted it to a wrought iron moldboard and wood handle. A farmer tried it and proved Deere's intuition right: Deere's new steel plow sliced through the soil without sticking. The farmer ordered two more.

Deere was in business. When his family arrived in Grand Detour in early 1838, it was to a different life.

By 1843, Deere had a partner in his plow factory. But this was not a success—few of Deere's early business relationships were. A later partnership led Deere and his factory to Moline, on the Mississippi River. By October 1843, the new factory had finished its first ten plows.

Deere took on partners almost at the drop of a hat and separated from them almost as

readily. His finances were regularly a disaster. The most beneficial partnership arrived in 1853: an affiliation with a young school-trained accountant, Charles Deere, his son. Charles enjoyed meeting the customers and demonstrating the equipment as much as his father did. Yet Charles also had the discipline to keep the business balanced and the accounts paid. So when one more reorganization headed off financial trouble, Charles was named vice president, in 1857.

Charles Deere acknowledged the ideas of his competitors and adopted them. Like McCormick, he opened branch offices. This expansion gave Deere & Company quicker response to its customers and better control of its cash flow. By the end of the nineteenth century, Deere & Company's line included cultivators, harrows, seed drills and planters, wagons and buggies, and even bicycles in the 1890s.

Deere adopted ideas from Oliver and Moline plows in his New Deal line introduced in early 1890. These plows were offered in single-bottom versions, and combinations up to six gangs were shown in catalogs. Although horses could pull two plows, something more powerful was in mind at Deere.

In 1889, a Deere brochure showed the New Deal six-gang plows behind a steam traction engine. The company had tested a steamer and advertised costs as low as 50¢ per acre, plowing up to 20 acres per day.

The new century brought a new business challenge. In 1902, International Harvester Company was created by combining several firms. At first, Charles Deere watched with interest, but since International Harvester and Deere had no product lines in common, he kept his distance.

International Harvester skirted Deere too, yet kept up its acquisitive ways. Rumors flew. One even suggested that IH was after Deere. But in October 1903, Deere learned that IH was after Dain Manufacturing, a hay equipment company in Ottumwa, Iowa. Dain and Deere had enjoyed a long relationship together, and Deere was worried. Dain immediately sold out to Deere and founder Joseph Dain, Sr., became a vice president.

The 1900s decade was hard on Charles Deere: competition, acquisition, expansion; battles against International Harvester. It took its toll. Noticeably ill, he continued to work until his death on October 29, 1907, at sixty-nine. He had

John Deere's Waterloo Boy signaled the arrival of the famous plowmaker in the tractor market.

run Deere & Company for fifty years. Under any threat to his markets, Charles Deere had consolidated Deere's interests.

William Butterworth, a lawyer by profession, became Deere & Company's next president. He was a faithful follower of Charles Deere's philosophies.

International Harvester still threatened. Deere had no harvesters in its line. A 1909 board meeting set out to acquire J. I. Case & Company. Case had harvesters and steam traction engines, another area Butterworth knew needed attention. The Case purchase fell through, but it awoke International Harvester to its own risk.

Another threat materialized as well. The automobile, a faint presence before the turn of the century, was ubiquitous by 1910. It brought farmers to town and town to the farmer. Although none of the implement manufacturers could imagine it, farmers paid cash for automobiles while they could only barely meet payment schedules on their machinery.

One account estimated that farmers had spent as much to buy cars as they owed to implement companies. Wayne Broehl, Jr., author of *John Deere's Company*, a thorough corporate history, reported the board's anxieties. Mechanization had come to the farm, yet the mechanizers agonized. Was the automobile unique, or would farmers jump to tractors with equal enthusiasm? Should they commit the development money to enter this new field?

In 1906, International Harvester introduced a tractor, and it owned the business by 1911. J. I. Case had produced steam traction engines since the 1890s and was working with Wallis to produce a gasoline machine.

In 1908, the Winnipeg Agricultural Motor Competitions began. Both steam traction and gasoline engine tractors were invited. In 1909, Deere was represented—as plows for the tests. Then in 1910, the Gas Traction Company of Minnesota's Big Four 30 hp won the gold medal pulling a seven-bottom Deere plow. A new consolidation was forged.

The next year, the machine was in Deere's catalogs, referred to as "our Big Four 30 gas tractor." While advertising it as a Deere product, the board investigated actually making it one. But Gas Traction rejected Deere's offer and instead sold to Emerson-Brantingham.

Deere's export department often marketed products from outside vendors. For Argentina and Uruguay, Deere demonstrated its ten-bottom plows with Minneapolis Steel & Machinery's Twin City 40 hp tractor. Deere saw more than ever the need for a tractor of its own.

Wayne Broehl, Jr., traced the history of Deere's tractor. At a board meeting in early 1915, a far-reaching decision was proposed: it must be "possible to divorce the tractor from the

plow and to thus make it available for general purposes." That Deere's tractor should do more than merely pull a plow seems obvious more than seventy-five years later. But at the time, when tractors themselves were still being defined, board member Willard Velie issued this visionary appraisal of tractor capabilities. Velie believed this flexibility would enhance sales. Deere's engineer C. H. Melvin was assigned to design and build a prototype.

Not everyone agreed. Butterworth had watched Rumely fall on hard times. The OilPull tractor's primary market was in Canada, and a crop failure there endangered repayment of countless tractor loans. That cost the Rumelys control of their firm, and Butterworth feared the same misfortune from something so uncertain as tractors. He had seen enough failed harvests and economic close calls. He felt uncomfortable with this expensive risk.

When Melvin completed his prototype in 1912, Butterworth must have felt relieved. Field tests were unsuccessful, and work stopped on the only prototype by 1914. The machine was a tricycle with power drive to two large front wheels. Designed for three plows, the Deere gang sat underneath, between the wheels. The center wheel trailed while plowing; the entire tractor reversed for hauling, with the center steering wheel leading.

But the board persisted. Joseph Dain was asked to work on a small tractor. The board knew of the prairie giants, machines weighing 10 and 12 tons, capable of pulling eight and ten plows. It knew too of the complexity and scale of repairs compared with the average mechanical ability of farmers.

The first Waterloo Boy kerosene tractor was introduced in 1914. The Model R followed in 1916, and the N was introduced in 1917. This early version is owned by Walter Keller of Kaukauna, Wisconsin. Top left, the horizontal engine was mounted transversely. Its starting crank was engaged on the driver's right, just ahead of the tractor's rear drive wheels. Right, the valve-in-head design meant no valve covers. But exposed rocker arms, common at the time, were prone to damage from dust and dirt.

The colorful Waterloo Boy logo. Right, the two-cylinder 6.50x7.00 in. kerosene engine rated nearly 16 hp on the drawbar. The Model N weighed 6,183 lb. and was the first Waterloo Boy tractor fitted with two speeds forward. Far right, the John Deere Model C was conceived for row-crop farmers. Rated 10–20 hp, production of the C was limited to fewer than 110.

board decided to continue development. By fall 1915, the second Dain was plowing near Moline, then on to Minnesota and Texas. A positive gear-drive transmission replaced the friction drive. Ten more prototypes were built using a more powerful McVicker engine.

Dain was asked to produce a tractor to sell for $700. With all-wheel drive, this new John Deere tractor could sell for $1,200. Most of the board accepted the price in view of all-wheel drive.

Butterworth fought it. He recalled Henry Ford and the millions invested in the Fordson in order to compete. Butterworth refused to squander the Deere family fortune on tractor development.

But Dain, still a board member himself, had patented his tractor in July 1916. Another year of testing convinced him of success, so in September 1917, he asked the board to build 100 for sale. Butterworth, by then a minority of one, held his peace, and production was authorized.

Dain died one month later—and Velie reminded the board of its 1912 decision to produce a small tractor. Now, nearly six years later, the company had spent $250,000, had produced twelve tractors and was behind a number of competitors. Wayne Broehl quoted a January 1918 Velie memo: "We cannot profitably make as small a number as 100 tractors. We should build tractors largely and whole-heartedly, or dismiss the tractor matter as inconsequential."

Velie had taken his own advice earlier. He had formed Velie Engineering in 1911. By 1916, his company had produced a four-cylinder tractor, the Velie Biltwell 12-24, priced at $1,750.

Velie galvanized the board. One Deere executive, concerned about the time span between manufacturing start-up and first sales, again suggested buying an existing company. The company making Waterloo Boy tractors, it was hinted, was available.

John Froelich's Iowa company grew out of his itinerant harvesting business, using a Case straw burner and threshing machine. By 1892, he had cobbled up a Van Duzen gas engine onto a Robinson tractor chassis. Froelich put it to work. It encouraged him to manufacture more. With partners, he formed the Waterloo Gasoline Traction Engine Company the next year. But of four prototypes built, only two sold, and they both came back, unsuccessful and unwanted.

Dain began in May and nine months later, his first efforts appeared, in February 1913. His tricycle followed the style of the day for "light-weight" tractors. Dain's machine was all-wheel drive, with chains propelling the front and rear axles. But Dain's steered the front wheels. The 3,800 lb. prototype worked well enough that the

Problems demonstrated during testing with the Model Cs resulted in most being recalled and reissued. This one escaped and is part of Walter Keller's collection. Below, what the number plate—Model C number 200,109—doesn't prove, the crudity of finish confirms: this is an experimental prototype, not a regular production model.

Froelich changed direction, producing only stationary gas engines. When even these did not succeed, he sold the company. The new owners renamed it the Waterloo Gasoline Engine Company. Two more tractors were built and sold, in 1896 and 1897, but Froelich's only interest was tractors, so he left.

In 1906, the name Waterloo Boy was adopted, and by 1912, new engineers had developed several tractors. The first, the Standard, was an 8,400 lb. 25 hp tractor. With a four-cylinder four-cycle engine, it used automobile-type steering.

By 1914, the Waterloo Tractor Company had built twenty-nine Model L and LA tractors. Nine were constructed as California Specials, tricycles. The other twenty were four-wheeled tractors. The two-cylinder engine for a new model, the R, was completed. About 116 of these were sold, designated Models A through D.

The alphabetical evolution continued. The final R Series model was lettered M, and it introduced the engine for the improved Model N. The R weighed around 5,240 lb. and sold for $985. The N, with a two-speed transmission, weighed 5,930 lb. and sold for $1,150. Waterloo produced a total 4,007 R and N Series tractors in 1917. All of them produced a distinctive *pop-pop* exhaust sound.

A report to the Deere board, quoted in Broehl's history, explained all the advantages of Waterloo's two-cylinders over its competitors' fours. Economy of construction, fewer parts needed to build or repair, and fuel economy were prime. But most appealing was logic: "Four cylinders are not necessary on tractors. The fact that a tractor is geared 50 to 1 instead of 4 to 1 eliminates all jerky motion. The engine of a tractor can be made heavy and have a heavy fly wheel and can be mounted on a strong rigid frame. Therefore a two cylinder engine is satisfactory in a tractor and when it is, why go to the four cylinder type?"

The purchase was approved, unanimously. On March 14, 1918, Deere & Company spent $2,350,000, and overnight it was in the tractor business. The 100 Dain tractors authorized in 1917 were completed by 1919 and were all shipped to South Dakota. But the Dain was doomed. Another effort, by Max Sklovsky, Deere's head of design, was also killed by the Waterloo acquisition. Sklovsky's tractor, another three-wheeled four-cylinder, had first

been tested in November 1915. A remarkable disaster—it would not turn—it did much better in a redesigned second incarnation. A smaller version, to run on a single cylinder, was interrupted permanently by the First World War.

Dain's second assignment in 1912 had been for a motorized cultivator. The air-cooled prototype appeared in 1916, but it was not strong enough for the work; it was a reversible, like the original Melvin. Refitted with the McVicker, it was called a Tractivator. Twenty-five were built for testing in September 1915. They were one-row units, distributed among Midwest dealers. But International Harvester brought out its two-row cultivator, so Deere's single was dropped.

Development continued with another cultivator designed by Walter Silver, a new two-row three-wheeler bearing a strong resemblance to Dain's tractor. Also underpowered, it returned to Moline for improvement, but 1921's postwar farm depression killed it. Yet these cultivators set the stage for "general purpose" tricycle-wheeled tractors. The general-purpose concept influenced tractor design forever.

In 1918, Waterloo had worked to eliminate wear of the final drive gear. An experimental model with enclosed running gear, profiting from the Wallis Cub design, was known as the Bath Tub. It did not succeed. Work continued after Deere's purchase; a roller-chain drive was finally adopted. The N was improved with automobile-type steering replacing the worm-and-chain system. The frame was no longer bolted together but was riveted by this time.

Experiments continued. Radically redesigned tractors underwent dozens of tests. Four styles were tried, again using alphabetical labeling. Something like thirty-seven test mules were built, each with a much shorter wheelbase than that on the N and R. Finally, style D was chosen for production.

The "tractor" had passed all second guesses with honors by 1921. Some 5,045 Waterloo Boy tractors had sold. A generation of farmers had learned to recognize the unique two-cylinder *pop-pop*. Company profits popped as well. Yet the satisfaction was short-lived; an upstart in the business, a manufacturer with only one

The GP ran 10x42.75 in. rear wheels on a 60 in. rear track. Overall it was 112 in. long and weighed a mere 3,600 lb. Right, GP number 204,213 was among the last four built, in mid-May 1929.

model of one kind of farm machine, threw the industry a curve.

Henry Ford believed that the depression was hitting farmers too hard. To keep his new Fordson tractor affordable and to keep production up, he would supplement losses on his tractors from profits on his automobiles. On January 27, 1921, Ford cut his basic tractor price from $785 to $620.

By March, International Harvester was hurt. It cut its price from $1,150 to $1,000, but its tractors still cost one-third more than Ford's. Deere waited, then twice dropped its prices. In July, the Waterloo Boy sold for $890.

Price war was war. In February 1922, Ford dropped the price to $395 and sales soared. But the floor fell out from beneath Deere. Seventy-nine Waterloo Boys had sold in all of 1921.

That Deere's tractor seemed aged in contrast to the Fordson was clear. A new tractor was a necessity. A last-minute debate argued whether to develop a four-cylinder engine—Ford and International Harvester both had them. Money ruled: it would cost too much. The new Model D would retain the two-cylinder engine. To be introduced early in 1923, it would sell for $1,000. Board member Leon Clausen suggested that 1,000 be built to start.

Hearts stopped around the table. Total tractor sales through 1921 and 1922 did not justify that kind of optimism. Yet, Clausen was wise. After a slow start, the Model D sold well; in 1925 it put the division in the black. But Clausen had left Deere by then, to become president of J. I. Case.

Don Macmillan and Russell Jones provided a thoroughly detailed comparison of Deere's equipment in *John Deere Tractors and Equipment*. Their major emphasis was on the tractors.

The first Ds differed from Waterloos by placing the steering on the left, directly linked to the front axle. After 879 were built during 1923 and 1924, the company changed from a 26 in. spoked flywheel to a 24 in. thicker flywheel of equal weight. A jointed steering rod, tested on some experimental tractors, was fitted into production machines. In 1924 and 1925, 4,876 Model Ds were built.

For 1926, a solid flywheel replaced the spoked version. In 1927, Deere export sales began: forty-six tractors went to Argentina and the Soviet Union. In the peak export year, 1929, Deere shipped 2,194 to Argentina, 2,232 to the Soviet Union. In 1930, a total 4,181 were delivered to Russians. For 1931, steering moved to the right side, with a worm-and-gear system.

The Model D again reminded Deere of its previous efforts with motorized cultivators. The standard tread designs pointed up the difficulties of mechanizing row crop agriculture.

International Harvester responded first. Its Farmall had higher ground clearance and greater rear-tread width than did its competition. With the front wheels nearly beside each other, it slipped between the rows. Farmall placed its cultivator out in front of the tractor for clear visibility.

Theo Brown, a Deere engineer with experience in all of Deere's tractor experiments, was asked to design the company's row crop all-purpose tractor in 1925. Brown bucked tradi-

The GP tricycle put usable information right in front of the farmer. The GP ran on kerosene and was equipped with three forward gears. Below, the horizontal two-cylinder had a 5.75 in. bore and 6.00 in. stroke. Rated at 10–20 hp, it was recommended for two plows.

About 2,000 Model BO tractors were converted to crawlers by the Lindeman company in Yakima, Washington. The B orchard versions featured flush-mounted engine air intakes, to maneuver under trees easily. The BO Lindemans were introduced in 1939, using the B 4.50x5.50 in. kerosene engine. Only 86 in. long without blade, the crawler weighed 4,420 lb.

tion: the new tractor specified a three-row cultivator while the IH Farmall performed well with either two- or four-row cultivators. By July 1926, the first three Deere Model C prototypes were ready as two-bottom-plow tractors.

Brown's immediate triumph with the C was a mechanism that used engine power to lift the cultivator from the ground. This innovation quickly appeared on all the competition.

Early trials worked favorably against the Farmall. Deere's dealers were impatient; the Farmall was already available and the Model C was still in development. But development pointed up problems—one of them insoluble.

In farming, the three-row cultivator configuration was less a problem than first imagined. But the Model C produced less power than the Farmall. And while Deere was still testing the C, International Harvester introduced an even more powerful engine. This embarrassed Deere's standard D as well!

In 1927, after the first five prototypes proved mostly successful, another twenty-four were begun, followed with another seventy-five. Dealers discouraged calling the new tractor a Model C—over a bad phone connection, *C* could be confused with *D*—so the General Purpose (GP) was created.

But more testing pointed out more problems. Although Midwestern corn growers got along well enough with three-row cultivators, Southern cotton growers disliked the idea. Also, the wide radiator and front wheel track caused visibility problems.

Brown and his designers returned to the drawing boards. An exhausting effort produced the GP Wide Tread (WT), amounting to a substantial redesign of the Model C. The GP-WT more closely resembled the Farmall. The GP went into regular production in 1928, and the GP-WT was introduced in 1929.

Improvements in 1931 raised Poppin' Johnny's horsepower. For 1932, a tapered hood improved visibility and allowed for an over-the-top steering system to reduce front wheel whip.

Even as they were solving problems plaguing the GP, Brown and his crew started on two new machines. The Model A tractor was introduced in 1934; the B came out in 1935. The A filled several Deere needs: a two-plow tractor, it offered adjustable tread width, the implement hitch and PTO shaft were placed on its centerline, and a hydraulic power lift system replaced the earlier mechanical system. Most important, the two-cylinder engine was reengineered to burn virtually any fuel: starting on gas, it was then switched over once operating temperatures were reached.

The B was described as two thirds of the A. This one-plow tractor shared every feature with the A, including availability with single front wheels, pneumatic rear tires and four-speed transmissions. The earliest As had an open shaft driving the fan, but this was enclosed for 1935, and all the Bs followed the later A style.

For 1937, high-clearance models were offered. Model A and B tractors also offered a regular configuration, with standard tread. Special versions for industrial use and for orchards featured fully enclosed rear wheels, independent rear wheel brakes for tighter maneuvering among trees, and air intake and exhaust stacks mounted flush on the tank cover.

Deere's tractors had been primarily utilitarian through the A, B and D. Early experiments had produced striking-looking bodywork on orchard models, frequently referred to as streamlined. But Deere engineers wanted all the machines more aesthetically pleasing. Independent designers such as Henry Dreyfuss had achieved recognition even from conservative companies.

Since the late 1920s, Dreyfuss and his staff had worked from his "yardstick of good industrial design," comprising five key elements: utility and safety of the product for the user, ease of maintenance, cost to produce, sales appeal to the buyer and product appearance.

Dreyfuss examined the A and B tractors, and in November 1937, when his version was unveiled, a new term denoting tractor history was born. Dreyfuss' group enclosed the steering shaft, incorporated a grille and radiator cowl, and in the bargain narrowed the whole for even better visibility. The effects enhanced safety and simplified manufacturing procedures. Deere's advertising referred to the new A and B as "Tomorrow's tractors today!" The resulting styling consciousness spread, and tractors that date before 1937 are generally referred to as unstyled.

Another variation of the B was designed specifically for West Coast needs. Some 2,000 Bs were converted to orchard crawlers by Lindeman Manufacturing of Yakima, Washington. This continued through 1945 when Deere bought Lindeman. In 1947, the Lindeman was replaced with Deere's Model MC, which was built in Dubuque, using tracks from the Yakima plant.

During this same period, another alliance was formed. An industrial Model D was introduced in 1926; hard rubber tires and high-speed gears allowed a top speed of 5 mph. Its commercial success resulted more from competitors' moves than from Deere's own marketing. Late in the 1920s, Allis-Chalmers had acquired Monarch Tractors, a crawler maker, and early in the 1930s, International Harvester introduced its

The Lindeman went anywhere—slowly. Top speed in fourth gear was 4 mph, but the crawler was three-plow rated. This 1946 model is owned by Robert Pollock of Denison, Iowa. Below, optional at extra cost, and now rare, the Lindeman hydraulic system raised and lowered the equally rare Lindeman blade.

The Model 60, introduced with an orchard version from the start, appeared in 1952.

first crawler. To California farmers, these two well-rounded competitors offered more than Deere—or Caterpillar—could match.

Caterpillar approached Deere early in 1935 and proposed selling both makes under one roof, thereby nearly doubling overnight the visibility of each maker. But another carrot was dangled to sweeten the offer.

In 1926, the newly formed Caterpillar Tractor Company had offered its harvester division to Deere. Caterpillar wanted too much then, but the passage of time had improved Caterpillar's offer and Deere's position. Caterpillar built harvesters only to service existing clients. So if

Deere would take over manufacture of the hillside harvester, Caterpillar would *give* Deere the division.

Deere had no hillside harvester of its own. It accepted the gift, and the arrangement was hammered out. The alliance continued through the 1950s, by which time Caterpillar was much more involved with heavy construction and roadbuilding, and its customers had less need for Deere's products.

The seeds sown by the tractor produced an unanticipated harvest. Because more work could be done mechanically than had been pos-

30

sible with horses, farmers took on more land. But for Deere, this situation pointed up a need for a more powerful row crop machine.

The 1938 Model G was introduced as a three-plow tractor. Where the B had been a scaled-down A, the G was scaled up. Henry Dreyfuss, otherwise occupied, got to the G in 1941. The modernized 1942 model resembled the A but sported a six-speed transmission and was now called the GM.

At the Moline Works, a small prototype tractor had been completed in 1936 and referred to as the Model Y, meant for the last holdouts working small farms with a team of horses. Successful tests with the 8 hp air-cooled Novo engine led to another twenty-three being built. The Y was updated and renamed the 62, and a small run of fewer than 100 was produced. When Deere had it right, it sold about 4,000 as the Model L.

The L broke considerable ground. The engine and driving position were offset from each other, better to see the work to be done and the row to be driven. It used an automotive-type three-speed transmission and a foot clutch. The characteristic two-cylinder engine was mounted upright. The L was only available on rubber. It was a lightweight, single-plow tractor, highly

Using the 5.50x6.75 in. engine, Nebraska tests rated the gas Model 60 tractor at 36.9 drawbar and 41.6 brake hp.

Designer Henry Dreyfuss' influence protected not only engine and mechanical parts from tree branches but also the operator's hands. Below, Robert Pollock's 1954 Model 60 Orchard streamliner demonstrates the effect of Dreyfuss' engineering and styling. The function of maneuvering through trees without catching the branches is less obvious than its contemporary space-age appearance.

maneuverable and easily affordable, and Deere recommended it to some buyers as their first tractor and to others as their second.

By 1939, Dreyfuss had produced a stylish grille and the quickly recognizable curved cowl became part of Deere design history.

A slightly larger LA, boasting 10 hp, was introduced in 1941. Both the L and the LA remained in production until 1946.

Upscaled from the LA but still well below the B, the 1939 Model H was the last nail to seal the farm horse's coffin. Styled from the first, narrow-track (HN) as well as high-clearance (HNH or HWH), versions were introduced annually. Offered only on rubber, the 13 hp tractor could run 7½ mph on the road in third gear by using its foot throttle to override the governor.

The Second World War came, and still experimentation went on so that when the war ended, new products were ready. A new plant was ready, as well; production began at Dubuque for a replacement for the H and L models.

The 1947 M introduced Touch-O-Matic hydraulics and the Quick-Tatch mounting system and reintroduced the vertical engine. Aimed at farmers hardest hit by the war, those who lost manpower or horsepower, the new M enabled the farmer to do without a hired hand.

The farmer's driving comfort was scrutinized, too. The seat was adjustable, air-cushioned and fitted with a padded seatback. Dreyfuss innovated a steering wheel that would telescope back 1 ft. for easier driving when the farmer stood.

In 1949, a new variation appeared. The MT was a row crop version with a rear track that was widely adjustable—from 48 inches to 96 inches. It was offered either as a tricycle with single or dual fronts, or as a model with an adjustable front-axle width. Electric start was standard on all the Ms; electric lights were optional.

Engines assumed greater importance following World War II. Before the war, the two-cylinder designs still held their appeal. But the farmers who had been to war drove four-cylinder jeeps and six-cylinder trucks. The two-cylinder poppers came up short.

The sound of the Poppin' Johnny had become a form of communication. The noise of a tractor under load was deeper, more metallic, and many farm wives could hear the progress of their husbands. An engine popping quickly at midday often signaled when to put dinner on the table.

Deere had reached the limits of reliable power from a horizontal two-cylinder that could still work between rows. The slower engine speeds of the kerosene burners produced less power than did the higher-speed, higher-compression gasoline engines. And the diesel, introduced and perfected half a century before, was a great success in Caterpillars and even International Harvester crawlers. The standard-bearing D had to be replaced.

Prototype MX tractors, with diesel engines, were given thousands of hours of tests. The R was introduced in 1949. Like the Caterpillars, Deere's diesels started with a pony two-cylinder gas engine. The pony's exhaust heated the diesel, making even cold-weather starting easier.

The R took Deere's two-cylinders to new horizons. Independent rear brakes were carried over from the M, as was the padded seat. But live PTO was optional, as was a new hydraulic system, Powr-Trol, operated from the driver's

seat. Aggressive styling emphasized businesslike power and efficiency.

Deere family planning arrived in 1952 when the 50 and 60 Series replaced the B and A tractors. All replacements fit progressive niches. By 1955, the new family was all in place and models from 40 through 80 offered horsepower from 17 to 46. Both upright and horizontal engines introduced duplex carburetion and cyclonic fuel intake to feed and mix the fuel and air in each cylinder. Options included gas, distillates, LPG and diesel in the 70 Series.

To further civilize farmers, power steering using onboard hydraulics was offered in 1954. Instrumentation was complete. Tread width was adjustable, in row crops or standards.

Then in 1956, the entire line was again replaced. Power increased and the designations added 20s: 40 became 420, 50 became 520, up through 820 and down to a new 320. Deere's advertising boasted "Power to meet every need . . . six power sizes . . . 30 basic models."

Some differences were immediately recognizable, such as the new stylish green-and-

The 1957 John Deere Model 720 High Crop towers over the southwestern Iowa landscape. The Deere diesel, introduced with the Model R in 1949, and the High-Crop configuration brought out first on Model Bs in 1937, approached its ultimate form with this special purpose-built tractor. This 720 is owned by Robert Pollock.

Gangly but functional, the high-crop tractors were meant for cotton, sugar cane and some corn applications. This Model 720 offered 32 in. ground clearance. Below, six forward speeds move the 8,470 lb. High Crop diesel along at 10.5 mph. With its overall height of 101 in., the 720 seems capable of seeding the clouds as well as the soil. Right, this 720 HC is powered by Deere's 6.125x6.375 in. two-cylinder diesel. The tractor rated 53.66 drawbar hp.

yellow paint scheme. Other changes were more subtle, such as horsepower increases of about twenty percent throughout the line. Power steering was standard from the 520 up. Powr-Trol sped up lift and drop for implements, which could take advantage of quicker maneuvering. Load-and-depth control accomplished Deere's interpretation of the Ferguson System for automatic draft compensation. Engine power could widen or narrow the rear track.

It also began the end of an era. The two-cylinder Poppin' Johnnys, were to be replaced. In one of the best kept industrial secrets of manufacturing, work began, sometime in 1953, on a new engine. Wayne Broehl learned some of the fits and starts: "Right away there was a serious miscalculation.... The first efforts concentrated on a V4/V6 notion. The V-design engine had worked well on the automobile, but the idea was flawed for tractors—the narrowness required of the row-crop tractor would not allow the requisite juxtaposition of the pistons. After months of work on the V, the notion was abandoned."

It took *Forbes Magazine* to describe the result: D-Day. "All day long the big planes buzzed in and out of Dallas' Love Field. They carried passengers from New York and New Dorp (Pa.), from Paris, France and Paris, Ill., from Seattle and Sewanee (Tenn.). When darkness fell on Monday, August 29, 1960, more than 6,000 passengers—the biggest industrial airlift in history—had been safely landed."

The next day, exhibited outside the Cotton Bowl and unveiled inside Neiman-Marcus, John Deere's four-cylinder engines stole their own show. Mounted inside the new 1010, 2010, 3010 and 4010 Series tractors, Deere's New Generation of Power promised 36 to 84 hp.

The board's fear of silencing the Poppin' Johnny, of betraying the loyal, was unfounded. The strongest draft horses couldn't keep the buyers away. Over the next decade, these tractors and their heirs sold more than 400,000 copies.

Deere—the company of the blacksmith, the expansionist, the acquisitionist—read the farmer right, once again. Devoted to the popper for decades, Deere the twentieth-century conglomerate repeated its history. Deere the nineteenth-century blacksmith had given the farmer, devoted to the cast-iron plow for decades, exactly what the farmer was ready for at the precise time the farmer needed it.

Chapter 3

Caterpillar

The entire West looks on a Best tractor as the automobile
public looks on a Packard automobile.
Philip Rose, *The Black Book*, 1915

The discovery of gold in Sutter's Creek near Sacramento, in 1848 may rank as one of the most influential events in farm history in America. The rush for gold relocated to California more people than any other event anywhere in history.

But that was only part of the significance. Those who raced West fled the drudgery of life back East, in Europe and even in China. The skills the immigrants brought with them by and large were not those of geologists or mineralogists. Few had experience keeping shops or teaching school.

Most were farmers. And when the Sutter's Creek gold harvest was completed, most farmers had not profited enough to return home. Now they were Californians. They were not far from Sacramento, Stockton, even from San Francisco. Some gravitated to the cities—those who were already disenchanted with their lot and who were disposed to give city life a try.

But thousands of others discovered the other gold fields of California. These lands down the center of the state reminded them of eastern Kansas, of Nebraska, of Iowa. These were the lands where the "gold" was planted—and it looked the same there as it did in the Midwest.

Within two generations, California farmers were cultivating 2½ million acres of gold. Harvesting this gold proved as lucrative as harvesting the gold at Sutter's Creek. Newspapers at the time advertised harvester rates up to $3 per acre, a total of 7 million 1890 dollars.

For harvest machinery makers back East, the only route to California for their machines was by ship around Cape Horn. The equipment was too large for the rails. Yet many of the new arrivals had used these machines and knew their capabilities, especially when faced with the vast acreage. It was not long before more innovative farmers built their own.

Daniel Best was born in Ohio in 1833. He moved to Oregon when he was twenty-six to prospect for gold. Having met little success, he worked as a sawmill foreman near Portland, then built his own lumber mill at Tumwater, Washington. Restless, he left Washington in 1869 to join his three brothers farming in Marysville, California, about 40 miles north of Sacramento.

When he discovered that they had to haul their grain into Marysville and pay $3 per ton to have it cleaned, he began thinking about trans-

The 1902 Best 110 hp steamer is owned by the City of Oakland Museum but it resides at the Ardenwood Historical Farm, Freemont, California. The giant, one of 364 built, stands 17 ft. 4 in. tall and 28 ft. long, with 8 ft. 2 in. drive wheels.

The Best stood 17 ft. 4 in. to the top of the stack. The fireman, Frank Presley, attended his duties down below, while Glen Christoffersen manned the wheel. Above right, the faded paint around the firebox. Far right, below the steam gauge is the oiler for the Marsh pump, a steam-operated pump to siphon water, or pump water into the boiler. The green sphere is its expansion chamber. The original cylinder oiler is at far right. It utilized steam to heat the lubricating oil for better flow.

portable cleaners, to "bring the cleaner to the grain," as he later put it.

The next year, Best and his brothers were in business. He had built three cleaning machines, and with his brothers, he ran those three machines. It soon proved even more worthwhile for Best to manufacture the cleaners than to operate them, so he set up a facility in Oakland. Business flourished, and Best built to capacity. With inadequate yard space to store the machines ready for delivery, he stored them on Oakland's side streets.

When the Oakland police complained, he took $15,000, went 10 miles south and purchased Jacob Price's works in San Leandro. An observant man and quick study, Best knew his customers were already figuring ways to fit

cleaners to their combined harvesters. So in 1885, Best's manufacturing career adapted. Within three years, he had 150 Best combines at work.

At virtually the same time, in 1884, Benjamin and Charles Holt were making wagons at the Stockton Wheel Company. The Holts had in 1864 moved to San Francisco from Concord, New Hampshire, and in 1868 established C. H. Holt & Company, a lumber and wagon materials company similar to the one they had operated back East. The youngest Holt, Benjamin, had remained in Concord to run the business. But in 1883, probably seeking drier climates for aging wagon wood, the Holts brought Benjamin out to open a facility in Stockton.

The Holts saw the increasing trade in harvesting machinery and quickly bought a few key patents. They expanded the Stockton plant, built prototypes to test, and offered their first combined harvester to the public in 1885.

Early combines required dozens of horses or mules to pull them through the wheat fields. And the racket set up by moving parts and whining gears frequently frightened the horse teams. Stories of runaway combines, of horses and drivers injured or killed, were common. Knowing his competition, Holt designed his machines without interlocking gears to drive the moving parts inside and out. He used link belts—chains with replaceable links—which could be quickly reassembled if one broke out in the fields. He even advertised that his "quiet" combine had caused no runaways! Holt also pioneered the use of V-belts, tapered leathered belts connecting the threshing cylinder shaft to its drive. By 1900, he had produced 1,072 combines, more than all his competition together.

The hills around Stockton brought about a significant Holt invention. The early combines—narrow, top-heavy affairs mounted on narrow-track wooden wheels—sometimes toppled over if the long wheat-cutting headers got too far off balance. Even before it tipped over, the grain would not travel properly inside a tilted harvester. Holt conceived a sidehill harvester, featuring adjustable wheel height and header angle so that the harvester box was always vertical no matter the angle of the hill. Word of this development spread through the West, and Holt shipped sidehill harvesters throughout California and to Oregon and Washington.

Even with Holt's evolutionary V-belts and link chains, driving the harvesters with horse or mule teams was less than ideal. Horses and mules had to be fed and watered, harnessed or turned out. And when they were all together and traveling smoothly, they still only made slightly more than 1 mph. A 1 mile section represented 26.4 miles with a 20 ft. header. Even with three or four machines working, 640 acres was an eight-hour day. And many California farms stretched for miles.

The steam traction engine had first appeared in the United States as the product of Obed Hussey and Joseph Fawkes in Pennsylvania in the mid-1850s. Steam traction appeared in California in the 1860s, built by Philander Standish and Riley Doan. Then in 1886, George Berry of Visalia operated the first steam-powered combine. The scarcity of wood and coal in California forced Berry's steamer to burn straw for fuel.

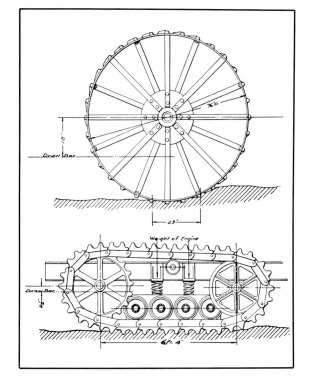

The advantage of a crawler track over a similar-size single wheel is made clear in this drawing. Given a wheel diameter of 6 ft. 4 in., the actual area of contact with the soil is only 23 in. The entire weight of the engine compacts the small patch of soil. A tracklayer-type tractor with the same 6 ft. 4 in. between drive wheel and idler axles, puts the full 6 ft. 4 in. down on the soil. Given identical-width tracks and wheels, the crawler weight is spread out more than three-to-one over the wheel.

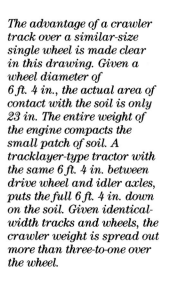

[doing] more work than 75 mules [and] costing less than 60 cents an acre [to harvest]."

By 1889, Benjamin Holt had produced his first steamer, nicknamed Betsy. Following through with his belief in chain drive, Holt avoided gears in his steamer. Friction arms operated the flywheels and the engine was reversible, but no transmission or differential was used. Betsy weighed a trim 24 tons but was reported to pull thirty plow bottoms and plant 40 acres per day.

Holt became Best's prime competitor, building similar machines, though Holt concentrated more on combined harvesters, whereas Best specialized in the traction engines. Although Best had built the first steam combine in the spring of 1889, Holt quickly followed and took a substantial production lead. By 1925, Best had built 1,351 combines, but Holt had built 8,000.

The two competitors' steam traction engines were also used in the Pacific Northwest to haul lumber from the stands of tall timber to the railhead. And both machines saw regular use in construction, towing large wagons.

But their primary use was in the planting and harvesting of grain. Working on soft peat, these heavyweights had extension rims fitted to the standard wheels to keep them from sinking into the soft watery soil. Tractor widths of 46 ft. were marvels but not uncommon. And so much power produced stunning performances. Stories are told of the Best machines, called the Monarchs of the Field, cutting swaths 50 ft. wide and clearing 100 acres per day. Other reports told of Holts cutting 5,000 acres in seventy-five days of nonstop harvesting. The fee for those performances, sometimes $1.25 per acre, paid for the machines in a single season!

The two competitors' prices were expensive for their day. Holt's engine went for nearly $5,000, his harvester for another $2,500; Best's prices were comparable. This precluded all but the largest farms from adopting steam power.

But even the magnificent steam engines with their huge swaths were not perfect. Their outrageous widths made maneuvering them more difficult than guiding two dozen horses. And horses did not spark and spit glowing embers. Harvesting at night by the light of kerosene lanterns was occasionally a fireworks show, even with spark arresters atop the smoke stacks. It became a large enough risk that insurance companies refused to insure California's exceptionally dry wheat during harvest time.

Jacob Price, the former owner of Daniel Best's works in San Leandro, was building his own steam traction engine in 1887 when he saw Berry's and was allowed to drive it. It amazed him how little work it took to harvest as much as 40 acres per day. Price returned to work, and by 1890 was claiming in print to have made the first steam traction engine.

Yet De Lafayette Remington, of the rifle-making Remingtons, held that he'd made the first, in Woodburn, Oregon, in 1885. His was patented in 1888 and demonstrated in San Leandro. Best saw it and bought the patents, upon which he quickly improved. The Best-Remington differed in many ways from the Midwest machines. Best's boiler was mounted upright, located at the rear between the drive wheels of a heavy frame. His machine was a tricycle. The two main drive wheels were 8 ft. tall and 30 in. wide. The drive was geared, and it was applied to the rim of the wheel, not the axle. The engine weighed 22,000 lb. yet produced 60 hp at 150 lb. of steam pressure. According to historians Reynold Wik, Graeme Quick and Wesley Buchele, three more engines were produced in 1889. One was capable of "pulling 60 tons along the road," another as "moving twice as fast as horses,

The steamer pulled 36 tons up a 12 percent grade. It was capable of drawing 36 7 in. plows through clay or adobe, at a rate of 12 acres per hour. The Best drove two 9x9 in. cylinders. Its water capacity was 940 gallons, but it used 125 per mile, giving it a useful range of 7.5 miles on a full tank! This steamer is restored and is still operated by volunteer crews.

THE
BEST
MANFG. CO.
SAN LEANDRO CAL.
No
185

41

Only two 45 hp Model Bs were built by the Northern Holt Company. But crawler tractors were less necessary in the Midwest where the first one was delivered, so it was returned to Pliny Holt's Minneapolis office. Far left, number 102, the earliest Holt crawler known to exist, was manufactured in 1909. Sold for $3,000, it was delivered to Tabasco Province, Mexico. Today it is part of the collection of Fred Heidrick of Woodland, California.

Fire danger was matched by the risk of explosion. Careless engineers, fatigued by relentless heat and long days, allowed pressure to build too high or water to run too low. Explosions resulted in dozens of deaths and led to state standards for boiler construction.

Holt's business grew enough that he purchased a satellite factory in Walla Walla, Washington, in 1902. By this time, he was already concerned about the value of farming the river bottom land in the San Joaquin valley. He knew that his 46 ft. wide steamers were too heavy and too inefficient.

Benjamin Holt was aware of tractors on tracks. In 1903, he and his nephew Pliny Holt toured Europe and the United States to see what had been done by competitors.

The earliest inventors of tracklayers had no practical applications for them, and with no motivation to continue development, they failed. Their successors did not have enough capital to

The 45 hp crawler's chain-driven steering system required plenty of forethought. Maneuverability was not an early strength of these Caterpillar predecessors despite steering clutches for each track. Right, external rocker arms betrayed the valve-in-head engine technology, literally; the swirling dust accelerated wear on exposed parts. The Holt engine was a 6x7 in. four cylinder and rated 25–45 hp.

fund further development, and they too failed, frequently after only their first or second tractor. Alvin Lombard, a millwright from Waterville, Maine, probably completed the first steam crawler to be a commercial success in June 1890.

Holt continued to worry about his harvesters and tricycle steamers bogging down in the San Joaquin-Sacramento delta bottoms where the richest soil could not even support a horse. Holt historian Reynold Wik surmised that since Holt knew of Lombard and other tracked efforts, he adapted his 40 hp Junior Road engine to rear tracks in the fall of 1904. Each track measured 9 ft. long and 2 ft. wide. The tracks consisted of 2x4 boards attached to one of his link chains so that drive sprockets would engage and move the chains.

It was Thanksgiving Day, November 24, 1904, that the steam crawler was first tested. Holt stood watching it with two friends: a painter, John Shepard, and a photographer, Charles Clements. Clements, briefly hypnotized by the motion of the track undulating across its upper guide rollers, observed aloud that it crawled like a caterpillar. Holt took to the name.

The keen competition between Ben Holt and Dan Best led first to a lawsuit filed by Best against Holt, charging infringement on Best's patents.

Losses brought appeals and retrials. But outside of court, the two sides were talking peace. And acquisition. On October 8, 1908, Best sold his business to Holt for $325,000. Both sides saw the end of steam power looming on the horizon. Having supported lawyers for several years, they agreed to settle—to combine assets and liabilities, dealers and technologies, and to operate under the Holt name.

The 1913 Best 30 "Humpback" used a drive gear above the independent idler wheels. This permitted manufacturer C. L. Best to lower the entire machine. This style may have resulted from a need to work under fruit trees. Left, the 30 was one of several styles available. Best called his crawlers "Tracklayers" and patented the term. Caterpillar returned to this humpback style with several of its current tractors. This tractor belongs to Fred Heidrick of Woodland, California.

45

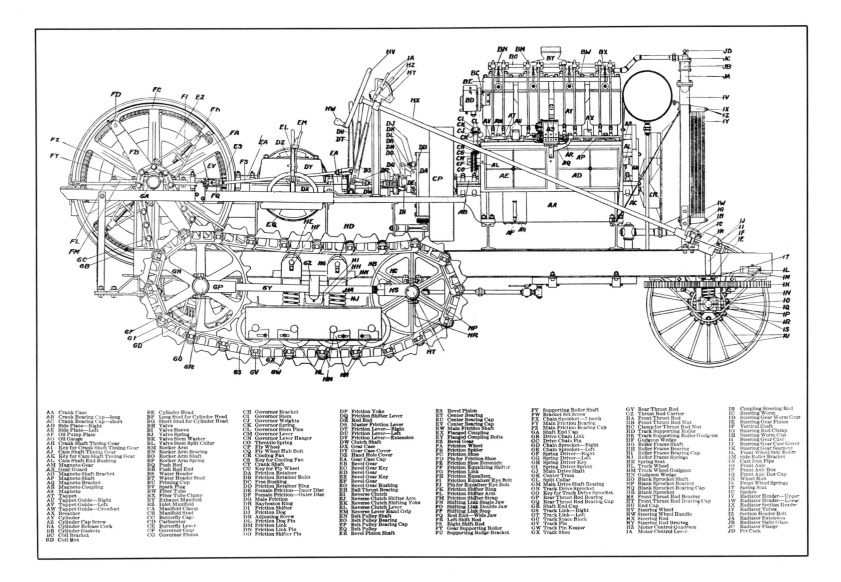

AA Crank Case	BE Cylinder Head	CH Governor Bracket	DP Friction Yoke	ES Bevel Pinion	FV Supporting Roller Shaft	GY Rear Thrust Rod	IB Coupling Steering Rod
AB Crank Bearing Cap—long	BF Long Stud for Cylinder Head	CI Governor Stem	DQ Friction Shifter Lever	ET Center Bearing	FW Bracket Set Screw	GZ Thrust Rod Carrier	IC Steering Worm
AC Crank Bearing Cap—short	BG Short Stud for Cylinder Head	CJ Governor Weights	DR Rod End	EU Center Bearing Cap	FX Chain Sprocket—7 tooth	HA Front Thrust Rod	ID Steering Gear Worm Gear
AD Side Plate—Right	BH Valve	CK Governor Spring	DS Master Friction Lever	EV Center Bearing Cap	FY Main Friction Bearing	HB Front Thrust Rod Nut	IE Steering Gear Pinion
AE Side Plate—Left	BI Valve Sleeve	CL Governor Stem Pins	DT Friction Lever—Right	EW Main Friction Shaft	FZ Main Friction Bearing Cap	HC Clamp for Thrust Rod Nut	IF Vertical Shaft
AF Oil Pump Plate	BJ Valve Spring	CM Governor Lever	DU Friction Lever—Left	EX Flanged Coupling	GA Shaft End Cap	HD Track Supporting Roller	IG Steering Rod Clamp
AG Oil Gauge	BK Valve Stem Washer	CN Governor Lever Hanger	DV Friction Lever—Extension	EY Flanged Coupling Bolts	GB Drive Chain Link	HE Track Supporting Roller Gudgeon	IH Steering Worm Cap
AH Crank Shaft Timing Gear	BL Valve Stem Split Collar	CO Throttle Spring	DW Clutch Shaft	EZ Bevel Gear	GC Drive Chain Pin	HF Gudgeon Wedge	II Steering Gear Case
AI Key for Crank Shaft Timing Gear	BM Rocker Arm	CP Fly Wheel	DX Gear Case	FA Friction Wheel	GD Chain Sprocket—Right	HG Roller Frame Shaft	IJ Steering Gear Case Cover
AJ Cam Shaft Timing Gear	BN Rocker Arm Bearing	CQ Fly Wheel Hub Bolt	DY Gear Case Cover	FB Friction Spider	GE Chain Sprocket—Left	HH Roller Frame Bearing	IK Steering Gear Segment
AK Key for Cam Shaft Timing Gear	BO Rocker Arm Shaft	CR Hand Hole Cover	DZ Gear Case Cap	FC Friction Shoe	GF Spring Driver—Right	HI Roller Frame Bearing Cap	IL Front Wheel Side Roller
AL Cam Shaft End Bushing	BP Rocker Arm Spring	CS Cooling Fan	EA Gear Case Cap	FD Pin for Friction Shoe	GG Spring Driver—Left	HJ Roller Frame Springs	IM Side Roller Bracket
AM Magneto Gear	BQ Push Rod	CT Key for Cooling Fan	EB Bevel Gear	FE Friction Shoe Eccentric	GH Spring Driver Key	HK Spring Seat	IN Cast Iron Pipe
AN Gear Guard	BR Push Rod End	CU Key for Fly Wheel	EC Bevel Gear Key	FF Friction Equalizing Shifter	GI Spring Driver Spring	HL Truck Wheel	IO Front Axle
AO Magneto Shaft Bracket	BS Water Header	DA Friction Retainer	ED Bevel Gear	FG Friction Link	GJ Main Drive Shaft	HM Truck Wheel Rod Nut	IP Front Axle Box
AP Magneto Shaft	BT Water Header Stud	DB Friction Retainer Bolts	EE Bevel Gear Key	FH Friction Equalizer	GK Center Truss	HN Gudgeon Wedge	IQ Front Axle Box Cap
AQ Magneto Bracket	BU Priming Cup	DC Free Bushing	EF Bevel Gear	FI Friction Equalizer Eye Bolt	GL Split Collar	HO Blank Sprocket Shaft	IR Wheel Hub
AR Magneto-Coupling	BV Spark Plug	DD Friction Retainer Ring	EG Bevel Gear Bushing	FJ Pin for Equalizer Eye Bolt	GM Main Drive Shaft Bearing	HP Blank Sprocket	IS Front Wheel Springs
AS Magneto	BW Fiber Tube	DE Female Friction—Inner Disc	EH Ball Thrust Bearing	FK Friction Shifter Ring	GN Track Drive Sprocket	HQ Blank Sprocket Bearing	IT Spring Seat
AT Tappet	BX Fiber Tube Clamp	DF Female Friction—Outer Disc	EI Reverse Clutch	FL Friction Shifter Arm	GO Key for Track Drive Sprocket	HR Blank Sprocket Bearing Cap	IU Spokes
AU Tappet Guide—Right	BY Exhaust Manifold	DG Male Friction	EJ Reverse Clutch Shifter Arm	FM Friction Shifter Strap	GP Rear Thrust Rod Bearing	HS Front Thrust Rod Bearing	IV Radiator Header—Upper
AV Tappet Guide—Left	BZ Inlet Manifold	DH Raybestos Ring	EK Reverse Clutch Shifting Yoke	FN Shifting Link Single Jaw	GQ Rear Thrust Rod Bearing Cap	HT Front Thrust Rod Bearing Cap	IW Radiator Header—Lower
AW Tappet Guide—Crowfoot	CA Manifold Clamp	DI Friction Dog Pin	EL Reverse Clutch Lever	FO Shifting Link Double Jaw	GR Shaft End Cap	HU End Cap	IX Radiator Section Header
AX Breather	CB Manifold Stud	DJ Friction Dog	EM Reverse Lever Hand Grip	FP Shifting Link Stop	GS Track Link—Right	HV Steering Wheel	IY Radiator Tubes
AY Cylinder	CC Butterfly Cage	DK Adjusting Screw	EN Belt Pulley Shaft	FQ Rod End—Wide Jaw	GT Track Link—Left	HW Steering Wheel Handle	IZ Section Header Bolt
AZ Cylinder Cap Screw	CD Carburetor	DL Friction Dog Pin	EO Belt Pulley Bearing	FR Left Shift Rod	GU Track Space Block	HX Steering Rod	JA Radiator Extension
BA Cylinder Release Cock	CE Butterfly Lever	DM Friction Link	EP Belt Pulley Bearing Cap	FS Right Shift Rod	GV Track Pin	HY Steering Rod Bearing	JB Radiator Sight Glass
BB Cylinder Gaskets	CF Governor Gear	DN Friction Link Pin	EQ Belt Pulley	FT Gear Supporting Roller	GW Track Pin Keeper	HZ Motor Control Quadrant	JC Radiator Flange
BC Coil Bracket	CG Governor Pinion	DO Friction Shifter Pin	ER Bevel Pinion Shaft	FU Supporting Roller Bracket	GX Truck Shoe	IA Motor Control Lever	JD Pet Cock
BD Coil Box							

Holt's brown tractors with yellow trim. Best called his crawlers Tracklayers. Holt had registered Clements' term, Caterpillar, as a trademark in 1910. And so the rivalry continued.

Best's Tracklayers bore remarkable similarity to Holt's Caterpillars. Cautious after the first suit against Best, Holt had tried to control the crawler patents. He had his lawyers trace the history and legitimacy of every prior patent, those of George Berry and Alvin Lombard in particular. Holt's lawyers advised that there was little value in buying the Lombard patents outright. They summed up Holt's own patents further, concluding that none was entirely unique or original. Holt's hope of controlling a monopoly faded, but then so did his worry of infringement suits.

Leo Best had done his homework too, and his attorneys had reached the same conclusions. But their advice differed: they said to purchase any Lombard patents that predated Holt's. Any question of whose work came first would be solved by ownership of the earliest patents.

Around this time Philip Rose, an independent tractor engineer, was hired by General Motors to survey all the companies producing tractors in the United States. He summarized months of travel and investigation in his *Black Book*. Best and Holt together occupied twelve pages of his typewritten study.

This side elevation drawing shows in great detail the important parts of a Holt 60, an early model with the tiller wheel out front for steering and balance.

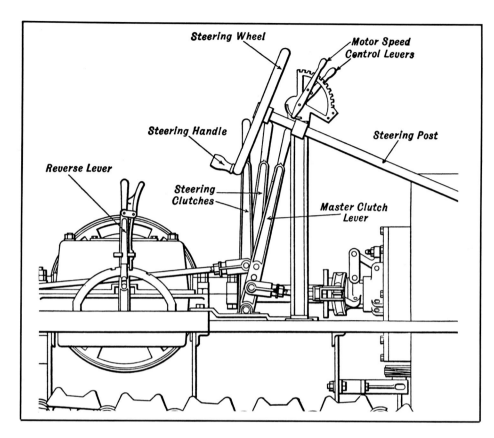

Steering Wheel

Motor Speed Control Levers

Steering Handle

Steering Post

Reverse Lever

Steering Clutches

Master Clutch Lever

Operating the Holt was all hand work and maneuvering in tight conditions was a handful of operations. With no track brakes, it was necessary to disengage the master clutch lever to stop all motion, but disengaging only one steering clutch would stop only the tracks on that side while the other side continued. Once the manipulation was mastered, subtle movements of the Holt were possible. Right, the 1917 Holt Model 75 sold new for about $5,500. That price did not include the Holt Land Leveller, which tractor owner Don Hunter has located.

His assessments of the mechanical differences were decisive: "The Best has developed many refinements which have been thoroughly proved out, while the Holt sticks to the old conservative design, always trying to improve their materials and methods but not changing or adding to the mechanism."

Rose described Best's system using a differential, whereas Holt "drives each side separately and eliminates the differential." Best had "a huge differential, which enables them to pull just as hard around a corner as on the straight away. They can out pull a Holt any time on a corner."

Both tractors were steered by power, and by this time, both had brakes for each track. "It's not necessary to use the hand wheel at all, except on a straight road. On a crooked road, it is much easier for the driver, as he merely has to move a little lever back and forth in order to steer."

Mysteriously, Rose uncovered a special Holt, one "for very marshy ground consisting of caterpillars only without a steering wheel. It is steered by throwing the caterpillars on each side into or

Under load, the Holt 75s easily demonstrated why they scarcely needed a front wheel. Despite its 23,600 lb. weight, under working conditions, the front wheel was often lifted above the ground.

out of gear. This machine is not cataloged, but it is about 40 hp and sells for $3,000. . . .

"I understand that they turned out only a few of this type for this country but that this was the type which was made to order and sold to Germany for their guns long before the war."

Whether this was the case or not, the First World War in Europe affected Best and Holt dramatically—and differently. Holt shipped crawlers—Caterpillars—off to the front, and Best shipped tractors around the United States. Virtually all Holt's production was picked up by the US Army. Best served the agricultural markets, and he had fifteen dealers by 1918.

After the war, Best retooled and broadened his line. By 1925, he had forty-three dealers and nearly twice the business he had five years earlier. Best tractors had profited from farmer input. His engines were reliable and well regarded.

Best's biggest tractor, the 75, weighed 17 tons, sold for $4,500 and was manufactured from 1912 through 1919. Just before World War I, Best introduced the 30, and in 1915, he offered a 6 ton Tracklayer 40, at $4,100.

Best's flexible tracks oscillated over small rocks and accommodated uneven ground without pitching the tracklayer from side to side. In

The view forward on the Holt 75 is like looking across the bow of a mechanical prairie schooner. But the noise of the 1,400 ci four-cylinder engine suggests much more speed is being made than its schooner-like 2.5 mph.

53

Owner Don Hunter of Ontario, California, operates his Holt-built Land Leveller while friend Bill Cox drives the Holt 75. Below, four cylinders, 7.50x8.00 in. each, produced 75 hp at 550 rpm. For idling, the engine could be slowed to the point where it nearly stalled—and one could actually count the revolutions. Far right, Benjamin Holt patented steering clutches to assist in turning his large crawlers. Other crawler manufacturers used differential steering, which slowed the inside track while speeding up the outside track. Holt's system completely disengaged power to one side.

1916, Best introduced the biggest and smallest of his line to date. A new 16 hp tracklayer was dwarfed by his new 90 hp 20 ton machine. The 90 stayed in production only through 1918, replaced by the Best 60.

Holt was an aggressive marketer himself. Before World War I, the US Army remained convinced only of the mule's ability to pull supply trains. Its experience with trucks led it to rule them out for materiel supply. Holt concluded a letter-writing campaign by finally offering to demonstrate his tractor anywhere at his own cost. By the time the US Army took a look, in May 1915, Holt had already sold tractors to France, Russia and Great Britain.

Holt's tests succeeded, and when the Army took bids on tractors, only Holt bid. By the time the first twenty-seven were delivered, Holt already sold more than 1,200 to the Allies, shipping his 75 hp Caterpillars to Europe. Sometime in 1917, however, he began to manufacture a new high-powered 120 hp six-cylinder. An erroneous newspaper account even credited Holt with the invention of the military tank, as a result of his big tractor sales to the English. It was a misconception, but Holt could not know the truth owing to the classified nature of the real information. And anyway, the publicity only added to Holt's reputation.

Holt expanded tremendously during the war, employing at one point 2,100 workers. The US Army ordered a total of 1,800 of the 45 hp tractors, 1,500 of the 75 hp tractors and 90 of the big 120s. Holt's war output was substantial. Historian Reynold Wik counted a total of 5,072, with nearly 2,100 sold directly to the Allies.

Holt's line-up suffered: he had no time to expand domestic sales, no personnel to service them and a limited line of products owing to the US government specifications. Peace treaties canceled all the wartime contracts, leaving Holt with large inventories, tractors ill-suited to agricultural needs and poor cash flow.

By 1920, the United States was in a depression. Wartime high production levels overtook the reduced demands of the postwar period. Holt was hit from both sides. Farmers who had needed machinery to meet wartime food demands lost their markets once peace came. Worse yet for Holt, the government, oversupplied with tractors, began flooding the market with war surplus.

When Ben Holt died in December 1920, he left a company reeling from its wartime successes but scrambling to survive. Holt's business manager, a former Boston banker, became president. Thomas Baxter ruled Holt with an iron hand, running the business with an eye to financial responsibility. He cut the large tractors from the line-up, introducing smaller models more suited to agricultural purposes. He learned of a $1 billion federal highway building fund and began directing company advertising to road contractors.

Thus, as Baxter spent money to revise Holt's line, the corporate debt increased. The result was a two-edged sword. With one swath it improved the machines and required full-capacity production to pay its way. Furthermore, Murray Baker, former vice president at Stockton, warned Baxter that Best was his biggest problem. As Philip Rose had concluded several years earlier, "From a mechanical standpoint and judging by the opinions of users, [Best] is the

The 1931 Caterpillar Model 60 number 1C1 sits next to a 1918 Holt 75, both part of the agricultural machinery collection at the University of California at Davis. Below, the first diesel used an auxiliary two-cylinder gasoline engine to start and warm the main block. Manually started, the crank is visible, just below this prototype's indentification number. Far right, Benjamin Holt's Caterpillar tractors first proved their worth in construction while working on the California Aqueduct through the Mojave Desert in 1908. By 1932, when the Panama Canal was dug, Caterpillar was the only way to go. This Model 60 was there.

finest and highest grade traction engine in the United States."

The C. L. Best Gas Traction Company was in little better shape. Leo Best had fought Holt's marketing trick for trick. He offered large trade-in allowances and favorable financing. Best's tractors had profited from continued development during World War I, but the fierce competition between the two companies was costing each severely.

Holt's Murray Baker met with Best's backers, Harry Fair, Oscar Star and Raymond Force, and together they combined and regrouped. Best and Holt again merged on March 2, 1925. C. L. Best and C. L. Neumiller from Best joined Murray Baker and Pliny Holt from Holt on the board of directors of the new corporation, the Caterpillar Tractor Co.

After the consolidation, Best's 30 hp and 60 hp tractors survived and were renamed Caterpillars. Best's forty-three US dealers were merged with his seven exporters. Total sales jumped up

Virgil Chritton, of Pomona, California, owns what is reported to be the last remaining Panama Canal construction Caterpillar, this 1932 Model 60. Far right, Chritton's Model 60 was converted from gas to propane power.

seventy percent even as Ford and International Harvester continued price wars to sell tractors.

Holt brought to the merger a worldwide reputation, plant facilities six times the size and sales revenues still twice the size of Best's. Holt also brought its 2 ton tractors; its 5 ton and 10 ton tractors were discontinued.

The four-cylinder gasoline engines, as the Caterpillar mainstay, were on final notice as well. The long-lived Best 60, born in 1919 and adopted in 1925, finally succumbed in 1931. A new engine, converted from gasoline, was out in practical field use, testing the theories of Rudolf

Diesel. A Model Sixty tractor, number 1C1, changed the sound and style of Caterpillars forever. The four-cylinder diesel engine displaced 1090 ci. In all, seventy-five of the first-series diesel Sixtys were produced.

In 1935, Caterpillar's model designations changed. No longer was tonnage displacement or horsepower nomenclature used as the model name, and no longer did that same number mark the radiator's sides. Rudolf Diesel's initials were paired with a number to describe the tractor's size. The RD6, RD7 and RD8 were followed by the RD4 in 1936. Standard gasoline engine

Daniel Best:
Development of the Diesel Caterpillar

"I can remember Dad telling me about Doctor Diesel in Germany. He had invented this engine that would run on anything that would burn—salad oil, alcohol. . . ."

Dad, in this case, was C. L. Best, Leo to family and friends. The speaker, his son Daniel, is now approaching eighty.

"Dad thought this was a good thing, that they ought to have it. But his colleagues were reluctant. They all said the company was doing well enough with the 30s and 60s. They didn't need to bring in anything new."

Dan Best was thirteen in 1925 when Best merged with Holt. He remembers conversations around the table a couple years afterward when his father, Caterpillar's president, went ahead and pursued his hunch about Diesel's engines.

"Dad heard about a troubleshooter in the East Bay who worked for the trans-Pacific shipping companies. When one of their diesel ships came in with troubles, they called this guy, anytime of day or night.

"His name was Art Rosen and when Dad got hold of him, he looked terrible, all pasty. You know, working all hours, day or night in dark holds of ships. Never saw daylight.

"He started working for us part-time. His assignment was to build a small diesel engine. This was unheard of at the time. Boat engines were great big things.

"Just about this time, Atlas brought out a diesel; it was a huge thing. At Caterpillar, they put one of the Atlases into a 60 tractor. They weren't too successful, though; they started with compressed air, so you had to have an air tank with you."

Perhaps Best's memories are so particularly sharp because he was never part of the firm. After the merger, rules decreed that no executives' family members could be employed. So, five years after the merger, at age eighteen he went farming. At first his dad was his partner. His recollections of the Caterpillar company came from years as an outside observer very much on the inside. He heard about it at dinner every night when Leo Best came home.

"Art Rosen's first engine was kind of a clumsy, big thing with about 50 hp. It had Bosch fuel-injection equipment. But the company didn't want to be dependent on Bosch so they set up their own manufacturing. Their engineers built all the fuel-injection equipment down in San Leandro for years. They were all Swiss watch makers. Very precise. I can remember going down there a few times over the years and you'd think it was a watch factory!"

It wasn't until 1930 that the company finished testing the diesel for itself. But Caterpillar also wanted the diesel tested under real conditions. So a couple of years earlier, Dan Best's father arranged for his son to use some for several years. He was to run it twenty-four hours a day, and record fuel and oil consumption, or any problems or difficulties.

"That diesel was hard starting sometimes. But as I recall it, it was Rosen came up with the idea of the gasoline starter engine.

"All the diesels were starting with air. The batteries were not so good at that time. Cold weather comes along and batteries have no zip. This auxiliary engine was something you packed along with you. At first it would have just been used to compress the air to turn over the engine. But then the idea came that it could heat up the engine. But even they were pretty temperamental sometimes.

"Actually the biggest problem you had was to break people into running them.

"When you got the gas engine running, you had to pull a manual Bendix by hand. Then you ran it a while to warm the big engine up. When you had enough power in the little engine, you ran it up and switched over to the big engine.

"When we were testing them, we'd get these old fellows. Couldn't get the hang of it. We'd run the engines twenty-four hours a day—in twelve hour shifts. The company would want to know how it would hold up continuously running. So these old guys, we'd start the engines for them. They'd run them, get them caught in a tight spot and kill it. Or they'd go to supper about midnight and shut it off."

Best's memory of those nights is sharp. A curious irony shimmers here like exhaust heat waves out a stack.

"Then when they had troubles and couldn't get it started again, they'd call us. So we'd have to go out and restart the engines for them. At midnight!"

But Best's job had one fringe benefit denied his troubleshooting predecessor Art Rosen, a man he clearly admires still.

Midnights when Rosen went to work, he labored under work lights twinkling in a foul, dank engine room. For Best, the twinkling light came from the star-filled skies.

With steering clutches and track brakes perfected, the Caterpillar 60 could turn inside its own length. Weighing about 25,860 lb., the 60 left a clear trail behind its progress. As a gas crawler, the 60 used the C. L. Best designed 6.50x8.50 in. four cylinder, running at 650 rpm. In Nebraska tractor tests, the 20,000 lb. gasoline 60 pulled a maximum of 12,360 lb. at up to 72.5 brake hp.

tractors were simply labeled the R Series. The designations were simplified further, to the letter D alone for diesel in 1937.

The next-generation line-up offered gasoline and diesel engines. The smallest D2 models sold for $1,725, with their four-cylinder engine started by its two-cylinder gas pony. The D6 used a three-cylinder, and the D7 and D8 were powered by a six-cylinder engine. The D8 was introduced at $6,950.

Ｔhe Caterpillar Tractor Company's experience and financial achievements led many of its agricultural competitors to think twice about crawlers. And some of them thought again after that.

Allis-Chalmers, Deere and International Harvester each made greater or lesser efforts to crack Caterpillar's exclusive, secure grip on the Western states' agricultural needs. Caterpillar's success in agricultural tractors may result from its specialization and from the corresponding desire to perfect the products within its specialization.

Agricultural tractor history is riddled with tales of makers awakening to the need for general-purpose tractors and then trying to become all things to all farmers. A barely contained diversity of machines led Allis-Chalmers, Case and International Harvester nearly to failure.

Henry Ford approached his business similarly to Caterpillar. Ford's Fordson was not the universal machine, but it sold exceptionally well because of its price and its engineering innovations. Had Ford not used his tractor as an experiment in farm and world economics, had he charged a reasonably profitable price for it, it is fair to guess it might have survived. His subsequent efforts with Ferguson prove that assessment accurate.

So, Caterpillar chose to perfect the tool for its own regional market. As an agricultural tractor, its machine worked best in Western soil. When Caterpillar moved its firm to the Midwest, it only briefly experimented with trying to make a Midwest version. When that failed, it didn't change the tractor for its new market. It encouraged a new use for the tractor, in construction, and changed to a new market for its old tractor.

Chapter 4

Allis-Chalmers

Every blacksmith in the country is building a tractor!
John B. Benson, advertising manager, M. Rumely Company,
La Porte, Indiana, 1915

It came together from disparate beginnings, blending the works of restless, ambitious, innovative men: James Decker and Charles Seville, Edward P. Allis and Meinrad Rumely. Their backgrounds in metalworking and machinery were the common threads.

One thread of the story began with James Decker and Charles Seville. Their Reliance Works flour milling company was founded in Milwaukee, Wisconsin, in 1847. For the next ten years, they manufactured millstones and associated machinery. Business grew. Expansion was necessary, and a 20 acre site was selected. But it would take new ownership to realize the progress.

The economy collapsed in 1857, and Decker and Seville were sold at a sheriff's auction in 1861. The buyer was Edward P. Allis, age thirty-seven, a businessman late of New York. Reliance had enjoyed a good reputation, and it didn't take Allis long to meet success. In fact, by January 1, 1868, he had opened an expanded plant at the site earlier selected by Reliance. The first Allis steam engine came from these new works.

The financial panic of 1873 caught Allis overextended, and bankruptcy followed. This time, Allis' own reputation saved him and reor-ganization was quickly accomplished, the company now called the Edward P. Allis Co. Allis' next move was to hire the best managers he could, the known experts in their field.

George M. Hinkley, a forty-year-old New Yorker, joined first. An inventive sawmill expert, Hinkley perfected the band saw. A thirty-four-year-old Scotsman, William D. Gray, joined next. Gray perfected the roller mill, revolutionizing the flour milling process. The third talent was Edwin Reynolds, who joined in 1877. This forty-six-year-old Connecticut native had been superintendent of Corliss Steam Engine works since age forty. He left Corliss in Providence, Rhode Island, because he was promised freedom to investigate his own ideas.

When Allis died in 1889, Hinkley, Gray and Reynolds kept innovating and business kept expanding. At the turn of the century, Allis was known as the largest steam engine builder in America. A new plant site of 100 acres was chosen; the West Allis plant opened in September 1902.

At this same time, William Chalmers, president of a machinery and stamping mill firm called Fraser & Chalmers, happened to meet Edwin Reynolds. Interest sparked in both men.

Rumely was sitting on top of the Americas as one of the most prominent tractor makers in the 1910s. Left, termed as one of Advance-Rumely's lightweights, this 1915 OilPull Model M weighed 8,750 lb.

"They brought us our meals on the tractor. We worked all day and slept on the tractors. It was maybe ten days before we got off the tractors." Bill Rohr's OilPull is now retired, like Rohr, and is visible at the Antique Gas & Steam Engine Museum, Vista, California. Below, the OilPull rated 35.39 hp on the pulley and was equipped with a three-speed transmission. The Model M sold for around $2,000 in 1915.

Allis was notably successful, and Reynolds had ambitions of additional factory facilities through which Allis would control the business of industrial engines. Chalmers' company was in trouble, and he saw Allis as a bailout. In turn, he could provide the additional plant capacity after which Reynolds hungered.

On May 8, 1901, Allis-Chalmers Company was incorporated, creating a conglomerate capable of suppling much of what American manufacturing might need.

Yet despite larger contracts, apparent successes and bigger, grander projects, Allis-Chalmers once again headed for financial trouble. The beginning of 1912 brought reality home, and a former Wisconsin National Guard brigadier general, Otto Falk, was drafted to take over. Allis-Chalmers Manufacturing was the new name. Falk, like many of the other financial reorganizers who had experience with Allis-Chalmers, recognized that the conglomerate had spread itself too far. Over the next decade, he closed four of the six plants Allis operated.

According to C. H. Wendel's *The Allis-Chalmers Story*, shortly after General Otto Falk arrived at Allis-Chalmers, he led a three-pronged attack on agriculture. He authorized a small tractor, a tractor-truck akin to the military half-track trucks to appear later and a tractor-tiller. This last project was accelerated by licensing a Swiss-built Motoculture rotary tiller. A tricycle apparatus, this featured a wide row of tines on a rotating axle dragged behind the machine. It cultivated deeply, pulverizing the earth, but it moved slowly, and this type of cultivation before planting was unfamiliar to American farmers. Wendel reported that it received little acceptance and disappeared as quickly as it arrived.

Falk's tractor-truck appears to be another misconceived idea. It appeared as a long-wheelbase flat-bed truck with crawler treads at the rear beneath the bed. It was meant to draw plows and carry loads. But again, a combination of elements killed it. Its proposed price was $5,000, roughly seventeen times the price of Henry Ford's Model A truck. At the time, Allis-Chalmers had yet to establish any kind of dealer and service network in agricultural machinery. This was an odd, expensive machine coming from a company that was simply unknown.

Gaar-Scott began building large gas tractors in 1911 in Richmond, Indiana. It was soon bought out by Rumely, who marketed the Gaar-Scott 18, 20 and 25 hp tractors as the TigerPulls. Far left, the Type M OilPull used Rumely's two-cylinder 6.812x8.250 in. engine, which featured the valve-in-head design. Tested by the University of Nebraska, it produced 27.54 hp at the drawbar. Below, "Who'd a thought a tractor has to be here 75 years for someone to want to write about it?" Bill Rohr, Compton, California, recalled that "I cut my teeth on these things."

TRADE MARK.

FATTENED
ON AN
AULTMAN-TAYLOR STRAW STACK.

Aultman-Taylor's logo showed a starving chicken that could be "Fattened on an Aultman-Taylor Straw Stack." Right, the OilPull 14–28 of 1918 was Advance-Rumely's entry into the "small" tractor field. Below, Rumely introduced its convertible tractor, the DoAll, in 1928. James Keenan was at the wheel of this DoAll on his Flandreau, South Dakota, farm in 1934.

History might suggest that persistence and nonconformism were words of daily inspiration to General Falk, because for the next five years, Falk's tractors were not accepted or respected. Falk's machines were innovative; for example, the first tractor, a 10–18 hp rated tricycle, was built on a one-piece heat-treated steel frame. Promotional literature boasted, "It has no rivets to work loose—will not sag under the heaviest strains." Yet its single front wheel was offset, which made steering difficult "under the heaviest strains."

The second-generation Allis-Chalmers tractor was the 6–12. It was conceived as a full-system machine, with its engine driving two large wheels under it way out in front. The implement of choice then also served as the rear wheel assembly. Its strong resemblance to Moline Plow Company's Universal prompted a note from Moline Plow about patent infringement. By August 1923, Allis-Chalmers had dropped the 6–12.

Ironically, Falk had succeeded nearly four years before. In December 1919, Allis-Chalmers brought to the market a stylish tractor with a 15-30 hp rating. Its smart appearance was at least somewhat inspired by current automotive designs. In profile, a continuous long line ran from the radiator to the rear drive wheels and circled down to the ground on the fenders. Allis-Chalmers reclassified it in February 1920 as the 18-30.

An accident of bad timing slowed the 18-30 to a complete halt within a couple years of introduction. The US economy had dug into a depression following World War I. Henry Ford reacted to the sales slowdown of his new Fordson by cutting its price by more than half. Manufacturers who could afford to play along with Ford dropped their prices too. But many who thought they could—and many who knew they couldn't—went under. C. H. Wendel reported that Allis-Chalmers sold 235 of the 18-30 in all of 1920.

Allis-Chalmers introduced a similar but less muscular tractor, the 12-20, in 1921. But it suffered badly from the depression and the tractor price wars, selling only 1,705 by 1928.

Life resumed when the economy loosened up. Tractor production was twenty times as great in 1928, the last year Allis-Chalmers offered its 18-30. Total sales neared 16,000.

Another thread of the story began in 1848 when Meinrad Rumely, a twenty-five-year-old German, immigrated to the United States to join his older brother Jacob in Canton, Ohio. Restless, he left to join his other brother John working for Russell & Company in nearby Massillon in 1850. But Meinrad stayed there only a few months. His itinerancy lead him to La Porte, Indiana. In 1852, he opened shop as a blacksmith, brother John soon joining him. By 1857, M. & J. Rumely had produced its first thresher, and in 1859, its machine beat thirteen others at the United States Fair. Rumely's first stationary steam engine came in 1861.

Rumely's stationary engines led to portable and traction engines. Meinrad bought out his brother John's interest in 1882 and renamed his firm M. Rumely Company. His traction engines were designed for hard work and long hours. Rumely engines offered optional extra water tanks and suction equipment. One principal drawback of steam power was fuel consumption: a full day's plowing required refueling. Self-

contained sustenance for a day's work seemed a distant goal.

Rumely knew of John Secor's experiments. Secor began in 1885 to work with low-grade distillate fuels in internal-combustion engines. He had tested a kerosene-burning ship engine at

Aultman-Taylor was founded in 1859 and built tractors such as the 15-30, left. By 1924, Advance-Rumely took over the operation.

the end of 1888. Secor continued with increasing success and notoriety.

Meinrad Rumley died on March 31, 1904. He was succeeded by his two sons, William, as president, and Joseph, as secretary and treasurer.

Bearing serial number U25–1, Allis-Chalmers produced a replica of its first rubber-tired Model U and presented it to the University of Nebraska for its collection. History was made at this site in 1934 when A-C offered its WC for testing on pneumatic rubber. Below, the Allis-Chalmers Model E, or 25–40, was an upgrading of the famous 20–35, arriving in farm fields in the early 1930s.

Joseph's son, Edward, age twenty-five, was also hired into Rumely company service when he returned from Germany. While studying for his medical degree there, Edward had met Rudolf Diesel. Diesel's theories appealed to the young doctor, but Edward saw no application for them.

When Edward returned to La Porte in 1907, he quickly grew into the business. A conversation one day about Diesel's work reminded William of Secor's engines years before. The similarities led Edward to find Secor. The Rumelys hoped to entice Secor to join them to produce a practical tractor engine.

Secor was a willing conspirator. He had already imagined automobile uses for his engines, and the adaptation to farm machines seemed a short step. Secor's nephew, William Higgins, had worked for him for five years while finishing school. This coincided with Secor's marine engine experimentation. Higgins left his uncle to satisfy his own curiosity about automobiles, and while on his own, he perfected the kerosene carburetor, which made Secor's engine workable. Because of Secor's tutelage and his help getting Higgins' invention patented, Higgins shared the patent with his uncle.

Thus when the Rumelys brought Secor to La Porte to begin working on the first OilPull tractors, Secor also brought Higgins. In his biography of Secor, *Power from Oil*, William Higgins' grandson William H. C. Higgins III related that the Rumelys acquired a package deal of both inventors and their patents for $213,000 in Rumely stock.

Within ten months, Secor and Higgins and a staff of designers completed the first prototype tractor. Higgins the biographer chronicled the accomplishments: "Starting with Rumely's existing steam tractor chassis [Secor] replaced the steam engine with a two-cylinder kerosene-fueled engine. The cylinders were mounted side-by-side and sloped downward from the cab area towards the front wheels. The engines were designed on the basis of . . . the use of water [injection] at heavy load."

Successful testing in 1909 led to production in early 1910. Although the shop crew came to refer to the Secor-Higgins prototype as Kerosene Annie, Edward Rumely and his secretary concocted the name OilPull. The first production OilPull was completed February 21, and within nine months, 100 had been turned out.

Edward Rumely's business efforts broadened further in October 1911 when he bought the Advance Thresher Co. of Battle Creek, Michigan. Advance Thresher had been established in 1881 and had sold something like 12,000 steam engines by then.

Rumely's 1911 buying binge added Gaar-Scott to his inventory. Gaar-Scott of Richmond, Indiana, founded in 1870, produced steam portable and traction engines, threshers and other farm machinery. Gaar-Scott had entered the gasoline tractor market the year Rumely bought it. Using a vertical four-cylinder engine, its 14 ton tractor was rated at 40-70 hp. Few were sold before Rumely took over, and afterwards only the existing parts inventory was used up. The Gaar-Scott Rumely TigerPull sold for $3,900.

C. H. Wendel reported Rumely sales in 1912 of around $16 million. Production was 2,656 tractors. Staff was around 2,000 employees. The two-cylinder Kerosene Annie went into production as the Model B OilPull. It was rated at 25-45 hp at 375 rpm and weighed a hefty 12 tons.

Rumely added Northwest Thresher Company in late 1912 and picked up Northwest's 24-40 tractor. Rumely reclassified the tractor as a 15-30 hp machine and named it the GasPull. It operated at a peak 600 rpm and weighed 9,000 lb. Rumely kept it in production at the former Northwest shops until 1915.

But 1913 was yet to come. Through the year, sales amounted to only 858 OilPulls, roughly one

The Model U sits on the test track at the University of Nebraska. Because of this machine, the University paved the formerly dirt oval in 1956. Above left, the Model U was first built under license for United Tractor & Equipment of Chicago. It first used a Continental 4.25x5.00 in. four-cylinder engine. Left, the Model U had three forward speeds, weighed 4,821 lb. and produced 19.28 drawbar hp. When tested on rubber, the horsepower didn't increase but the drawbar test weight increased 15 percent, fuel economy 25 percent and rider comfort increased immeasurably.

third of 1912's boom year total. Rumely was already heavily in debt to banks because of the acquisitions. With receipts drastically slowed owing to a disastrous crop failure in Canada, the banks got nervous and refused to extend credit.

And 1914 followed with even worse results. Dr. Edward Rumely resigned January 1, 1914. The stock offered Secor and Higgins had been valued at $100 per share. By the end of 1914, when only 357 OilPulls had sold, the stock was not moving at $22 per share.

In January 1915, M. Rumely Co. filed bankruptcy. The court appointed Finley Mount, a forty-eight-year-old Indianapolis lawyer, as receiver, and he quickly wielded the hatchet that trimmed up the Rumely empire. What was left was the former Advance Thresher factory in Battle Creek and the La Porte facilities of Rumely. What was born was the Advance-Rumely Company. Secor and Higgins had lost fortunes but returned to work; the Rumely family lost its fortune and the firm as well.

Development resumed on new tractors, and for 1918, the 15-30 introduced a high-tension magneto and optional spark plugs, which increased its power rating to 18-35. A 14-28 was introduced; its two-cylinder engine ran at 530 rpm. Both of these were one-year issues, the former being discontinued by 1920, the latter being increased to a 16-30 hp rating.

For Advance-Rumely, the Ford and International Harvester tractor prices wars had been hard to weather. But in October 1924, Advance-Rumely introduced a new series of lightweight OilPulls. The new 15-25 L weighed 6,000 lb. and introduced a new Advance-Rumely patent, the locking differential. In addition, all the gears in the L were completely enclosed and the transmission ran in ball bearings.

A Model R 25-45 and an M 20-35 joined the L, as did a new larger S 30-60. All these were improved for 1928. The lightweights gained power when engine modifications allowed an extra 100 rpm engine speed. The L 15-25 became the W 20-30, the M 20-35 became the X 25-40, the R 25-45 became the Y 30-50 and the S 0-60 grew into the Z 40-60.

Few of these "lightweights" were produced. Advance-Rumely had acquired the Toro Motor Cultivator rights in 1927. This led to the Do-All, introduced in 1929, Advance-Rumely's first *true* lightweight. This also attempted to fulfill the demand for an all-purpose tractor.

The Do-All was offered in convertible (from tractor into cultivator) and nonconvertible forms. By removing the front wheels and axle and rotating the rear axle hubs, a new center of gravity was set and higher ground clearance was achieved. Stability came with the necessary addition of a caster-type rear wheel. All the steering and control levers were fitted with extensions. It was advertised that this change-

Records indicate this replica was completed by Allis-Chalmers soon after the first Model U was equipped with pneumatic rubber tires. This is part of the Tractor Test Museum collection at the first tractor test facility in Lincoln, Nebraska. Right, Lester Larsen, at right, engineer-in-charge of University of Nebraska Tractor Testing for nearly 30 years, works with Raymond Beckner to correct a detail on the 1931 Allis-Chalmers Model U.

over could be accomplished in an afternoon. It remained in production through 1931.

Late in 1929, Finley Mount approached General Otto Falk. Then Dr. Edward Rumely returned after a disastrous newspaper ownership career in New York, and he became involved in new merger plans in January 1930. Rumely eloquently "sold" the merger, explaining the advantages to Falk. An $8 million sum in outstanding farmer loan notes was characterized as a benefit to Falk, but to his board it was worrisome. Yet on June 1, 1931, Advance-Rumely was absorbed into Allis-Chalmers. Allis-Chalmers thereby became the fourth-largest farm equipment maker in the United States.

As the Advance-Rumely inventories were used up, all the company's tractors went out of production.

Generation Otto Falk had taken a beating during the first half of his two decades with Allis-Chalmers. In force-feeding tractors to the company, he had made mistakes and cost Allis-Chalmers money. Still he persevered. By 1926, the tractor department was well established and another bright talent, Harry C. Merritt, was brought in.

By all accounts, Merritt was a progressive innovator. He seemed to look on the tractor department from anywhere but the traditional historical perspective. As department manager, he could move Allis-Chalmers' tractors forward, and with the tractor department being General Falk's favorite son, Merritt received the encouragement as well.

The new 20-35, introduced in 1929, was a slightly improved version of its predecessor, the 18-30. Also known as the Model L, it was available for only two years. Meanwhile, a new tractor was being prepared by Allis-Chalmers for an outside marketing firm, United Tractor & Equipment of Chicago.

A three-plow-rated machine, the tractor used a four-cylinder Continental engine. When United failed despite seemingly adequate support and backing, Allis-Chalmers continued to sell the tractor, shortening the name to Model U.

During this same time, Merritt had traveled west. Visiting California in the spring, he was startled and impressed by the wild poppies covering the hillsides. Their bright orange color struck him. Returning to Milwaukee, he must have reflected on the somber green tractors his

department produced. Persian Orange most closely matched the wild fields of California, and it didn't take much time before Merritt's Persian Orange tractors covered the furrowed fields of the Midwest.

The Persian Orange U remained in production through 1944, and Allis-Chalmers built more than 10,000 of them. Continental engines powered the early Us until Allis-Chalmers' own UM four-cylinder engine appeared in 1933. The U was offered in a variety of styles, including the Ind-U-strial, a crawler, a railroad yard switcher built by Brookville Locomotive and a row crop version. But it was not its longevity, its adaptability or even its new color for which Allis-Chalmer's Model U was most famous. It was Harry Merritt's friendship with Harvey Firestone.

Alfred Lief, in his 1951 history *The Firestone Story*, categorized Firestone's innovation as one of the company's "self-helps to recovery" from the preceding decade of financial depression. It was that at the very least.

Firestone's family farm, the Homestead, ran on steel. Merritt, a family friend, had offered Firestone one of Allis-Chalmers' new Model U tractors. Firestone, long convinced of the value of pneumatic tires on the road, wondered about their application to the farm. Surely, the same economy of operation, the same operator comfort, the same reduction in vibration would

A 1936 Allis-Chalmers WC at work pulling an All-Crop harvester. The WC was one of Allis-Chalmers most successful models ever, with a total of some 178,202 units built between 1934 and 1948.

The Persian Orange paint of this 1933 Model M has faded from years in the southern California sun. The Allis-Chalmers Model M crawler number 1 now resides at the Antique Gas & Steam Engine Museum in Vista, California. Built for the Los Angeles County Department of Parks and Recreation, it ended its working years at Griffith Park in Los Angeles.

apply . . . if the problem of traction could be solved.

Lief explained Firestone's conviction: "His was the enthusiasm that inspired coworkers, and they tackled the problem with the same blend of tingle of excitement and steadiness of purpose. The tire must have a high diameter, demanded by the clearance of a tractor in farm operations, and a wide cross section for contact with the soil and fit in furrow. This contact must be firm so the tractor might pull without power loss yet the grip must not cause the tire to creep on the rim. Excessive air pressure would pack the soil too hard; insufficient pressure would allow slipping on the rim.

"In the original development work, flat truck rims were used. Airplane tires in sizes 6.50x16 and 11.25x24 were mounted on them. They rim-crept. The answer was a drop-center rim with a tight bead fit. So much for creepage. As for traction, the tread must bite into earth, sand, wet clay, sod, but chevrons cut too deep would bend under the load, that is, if unsupported. And this necessity gave birth to the idea of a connected bar design—the continuation of one side of a chevron to the bar above it."

Firestone's Homestead Farm was completely re-tired; every tractor and implement was changed over to his new Ground Grip pneumatic. And Merritt changed the specifications on his Model U. Inflatable rubber was offered as

an option. To promote some of the virtues of the new tires, Firestone and Merritt coaxed Indianapolis racer Barney Oldfield out of retirement and put him back on the county fair race circuit—on a rubber-shod Model U. *Implement & Tractor* magazine reported countless events. In five-lap races against local Allis-Chalmers owners and salespeople, Oldfield would let the local amateurs lead for the first four laps then sprint past them showing off the speed and traction capabilities of the combination. Merritt had fitted especially high "road" gears to the racers; on one top-speed run, Oldfield set a record of more than 64 mph with a specially modified U and Firestone's inflatables.

Merritt's brightly colored rubber-shod tractors garnered attention even as farmers acknowledged the uselessness of 64 mph machines. The Model U became the first tractor in the United States offered with rubber. When Merritt introduced Allis-Chalmers' second-generation row crop, the WC, in 1934, it was the first tractor to be designed with inflatable rubber specified as standard equipment. Curiously, perhaps to placate conservative farmers, steel wheels were optional, even through the 1940 introduction of the WF standard-tread version of the WC. World War II returned some of the U, WC and WF models to steel, but once the war ended, steel wheels were no longer offered.

The eventual success of Merritt and Falk with their tractors was due in no small part to the full line of implements offered for each machine. Mechanical farming was available for every crop with Allis-Chalmers. And virtually every size farm was served after the 1937 introduction of its lightweight Model B. A fully optioned 1940 Model B weighed less than 1,900 lb. and sold for $570. The Model C introduced distillate fuel engines in 1940. The narrow-front-tire configuration was rated as a two-plow tractor and also introduced Allis-Chalmers' Quick-Hitch system for rapid attachment and release of cultivators and other equipment.

A new system of implements and a small tractor were introduced in 1948 with the rear-engined Model G, rated 9.6–10.6 hp and Allis-Chalmers' smallest to date. The Model B rated 10–14 hp out of the four it shared with the C.

The 1948 WD tractor introduced the Traction-Booster, a three-point hydraulic hitch and a hand clutch to stop tractor motion. The WDs were offered in single, narrow and standard front ends, through 1953. That year, Allis-Chalmers introduced its Snap-Coupler system, a more versatile replacement to the Quick-Hitch. The WD's replacement was a more powerful version, the WD-45. An LPG version was offered from the start. In addition, Allis-Chalmers' WD-45 was the first tractor to offer factory-installed power steering.

It was not until 1955 that Allis-Chalmers had a diesel in its line. The WD-45 diesel used a new six-cylinder 230 ci engine.

In 1957, an entire new line of tractors cleared the boards. The D-14 and D-17 tractors were introduced at $2,875 and $3,550, respectively. The D-14 used a four of Allis-Chalmers' own design and was available in gas or LPG; the D-17 gas was also a four and the D-17 diesel was an enlarged six of 262 ci.

The D-14 and D-17 introduced many new features. A Roll-shift front axle used the power steering system to change front track, much the same as its rear axles did. A Power Director added a high range to each transmission gear.

General Otto Falk served as Allis-Chalmers' president from its reorganization in 1913 through 1931. Falk's legacy was the placement of Allis-Chalmers onto solid financial ground and into solid contention as a leading farm equipment manufacturer.

Max Babb replaced Falk as president and continued with Falk's well-set direction. Walter Geist, who developed Allis-Chalmers' Texrope multiple V-belt drive system, was named president in 1942, remaining until 1951. W. A. Roberts then served a short four years and worked to tighten up Allis-Chalmers' loose organization. His successor, Robert Stevenson, took office in 1955.

His successor, David Scott, split Allis-Chalmers' tractor division off, giving it independence. The division enjoyed success until 1980, when the previously swelling agricultural equipment balloon began to shrivel. On March 28, 1985, an agreement between principals sold Allis-Chalmers Agricultural Equipment Group to a subsidiary of Klockner-Humboldt-Deutz AG of West Germany.

The last name change was introduced. The last color change was ordered. Deutz-Allis was born. Persian Orange was resprayed Deutz Green.

In 1990, Harry Merritt's legacy returned. Allis' sales had diminished some, the partial result of an unfamiliar color on a somewhat familiar name. In April, the original Allis-Chalmers Agricultural Equipment Group was re-acquired from Deutz-Allis by a group of American investors including company officials. By July the new American management, while retaining Deutz-Allis' name, had reinstated Allis' signature corporate Orange on all domestic-manufactured machines.

Track brakes, track clutches, gear shift and hand throttle were standard on the Model M. The museum staff at Vista added the kill switch. Below, the 1933 Model M used an Allis-Chalmers four-cylinder gasoline engine with 4.375x5.00 in. bore and stroke. Its Nebraska test produced 29.65 hp. It weighed 6,620 lb.

Chapter 5

Case

The large thresher companies must all be considered as strong, aggressive competitors in the tractor business. They have the advantage of being established in the farm trade, of having branch houses and a trained sales force. They are not strong originators but are excellent copyists.
Philip Rose, *The Black Book*, 1915

Jerome Increase Case was twenty-three when he left home. He moved west, to Wisconsin, taking with him six Groundhog threshers, purchased on credit. He settled near Racine, some 30 miles south of Milwaukee.

Born in Williamstown, New York, on December 11, 1819, he grew up assisting his father operating and selling threshers. Jerome's lifelong experience with threshers helped him sell his first five. His industriousness made him keep the sixth, to work with and earn money. Later, his curiosity took over and the sixth became his test bed. His work evolved into a harvester, which combined threshing with cleaning, separating the wheat completely from the chaff. By late 1844, he had perfected his new harvester and was producing it in Racine.

During the next three years, he expanded his shops as demand for his machines increased. In 1863, his twentieth year in business, he incorporated J. I. Case & Company, naming his brother-in-law Stephen Bull vice president. Case's Racine Threshing Machine Works joined about 200 other companies manufacturing har-

vesters. At the end of the Civil War, he adopted the company logo, Old Abe, the eagle. It was Wisconsin's state bird and had been the battlefield emblem of the 8th Wisconsin Regiment from Eau Claire.

Case continually improved his machines. He regularly adopted ideas from his competitors: Hiram and John Pitts, Hiram Moore, John Cox and Cyrus Roberts, Cyrus McCormick. In 1869, Case introduced a portable steam engine to replace horse-powered treadmills and rotary sweeps. Case's reputation for quality and innovation continued with the steamer, and it sold well for decades.

In 1884, Case brought out his first steam traction engine. The direct-flue-type boiler provided motion, but horses were still needed to steer it. Soon after, a steering wheel was attached to a worm gear and chains to pull the front axle left or right. Case ultimately produced steam traction engines as large as 150 hp and as late as 1924. Only nine of the giant 150 hp machines were produced from 1905 through

"Old Abe," the bald eagle that was the symbol of J. I. Case for decades. Left, the Model LA was Case's most powerful tractor in 1948, rated at 55.6 brake hp in a 1952 Nebraska test. This Model LA is owned by Cliff Feldkamp of Kaukauna, Iowa.

The Gas Traction Company's Big Four 30 won the gold medal in 1911 at the Winnipeg, Canada, tractor tests, a forerunner to the Nebraska tests. Right, by 1912, Emerson-Brantingham had bought out the Gas Traction Company and the Big Four 30 appeared under the E-B logo. This is the firm's revised version, the 20–35 tractor of 1913.

Fill the Broken Ranks of Farm Labor With

E-B 12-20 Kerosene Tractors

WHEN the men leave the fields to fight for democracy, fill their places with the power that has been proven most efficient and adaptable to present conditions.

E-B 12-20 Tractors were the first selected to be operated by crippled French soldiers on the shell-torn fields of France. They are the choice for the average American farm. The Automobile type steering equipment and control and four-cylinder motor make them simple and easy for a woman or boy to operate.

25% more power on the drawbar this year puts the E-B 12-20 in a class by itself.

Other E-B Tractors, the 9-16, 20-35, 40-65, enable you to have E-B advantages in tractor work whatever the size of your farm. All have E-B standardized features. All 4-wheels, 4-cylinder, kerosene burning.

Ask your E-B dealer for our big tractor catalog or write us.

Increase your crop yields by using labor-saving farm machinery. Look for it under the E-B trademark. It shows the way to better, more profitable farming. Ask your dealer for E-B Implements or write us.

EMERSON-BRANTINGHAM IMPLEMENT CO., INC.

Good Farm Machinery   **Rockford, Illinois**   *Established 1852*

Your Problem—To increase crops with decreased help. Your Remedy—E-B Tractors and Labor-Saving Farm Machinery

Emerson-Brantingham was formed in 1909, and constructed a line of tractors until it was purchased by Case in 1928. The Model Q 12–20 arrived in 1917, helping on the farm when the men went off to fight the Great War.

John Heider had been an Iowa farmer before he moved to building tractors. His Heider tractor line was teamed with the Rock Island brand plows in a strong selling agreement, far right. The 1915 Heider Model C weighed nearly 6,000 lb. and sold new for about $1,100. Below, the operator started the engine on gasoline and then switched over to kerosene when it was warm.

1907. Each weighed 18 tons dry and sold for $4,000.

Jerome Case died December 22, 1891, and Stephen Bull succeeded him. The next year, the company's first gas engine tractor was tested. Alan King, in his *J. I. Case 1918–1959*, quoted David Pryce Davies, who at the time was a draftsman working in Case's experimental department: "The engine was of the four-cycle type. . . . Very little was known at this early date regarding either carburization or ignition and there was not a single manufacturer of carburetors or apparatus pertaining to ignition. . . . Because of the lack of proper carburetor and ignition it was decided to drop the tractor at that time." Davies went on to become vice president of engineering at Case.

In 1901, Stephen Bull's son Frank became president. The desire for smaller tractors continued even as Case's steam traction engines proliferated; a total of 35,838 were sold by the end of steamer production in 1924. By 1911, however, Case had solved the problems of fuel mix and spark, and it introduced the 30-60.

The 30-60's descendance from Case steam traction engines is obvious. Its resemblance to early Hart-Parr machines is no coincidence either, since Hart-Parr had produced and sold successful gas engines just as Frank Bull was taking over for his father. Yet Case was one of the quickest to achieve acclaim, winning first place at the 1911 Winnipeg Tractor trials.

For regular production begun in 1912, the radiator shape and configuration were changed substantially, but the 30-60 continued in production through 1916. The tractor's horizontal two-cylinder engine reached peak power at 365 rpm. It sold for $2,500.

A compact version was introduced in 1913. It rated 12-25 hp from its two-cylinder engine and sold for $1,350. A 20-40 hp midrange tractor was also introduced. Another successful machine, this won two gold medals at the 1913 Winnipeg trials. An 8x9 in. opposed two-cylinder engine, like many early gas engines, used exhaust to induce airflow over the radiator. Eventually, this system was replaced by a water pump and fan.

In the mid-1910s, farmers became intrigued by three-wheelers. Case responded with its 10-20 in 1915. More significant was its first vertical-mount four-cylinder engine. The engine, fitted transversely across the cast frame, was fully enclosed.

Case reacted to competition from International Harvester and Wallis by introducing its compact 9-18 in 1916. The same year saw Case's fourth president elected, Warren J. Davis.

The next cross-mount cast-frame Case was the 15-27, introduced at the end of 1918. The engine differed by being cast with all four cylinders in the same casting. The engine breathed through an early water-bath air cleaner. The tractor weighed about 6,400 lb. and sold for $1,800.

The largest of the Case line-up arrived at the beginning of 1920 and was rated a 22-40 hp tractor. Similar to the 9-18 and 15-27 was its crosswise-mounted four-cylinder; dissimilar, however, was the frame. Case reverted to channel iron built up and assembled rather than the one-piece castings on the smaller machines.

Constant upgrading was Case's goal, and continued prizes in worldwide competitions provided the motivation. Case's 10-20 tricycle

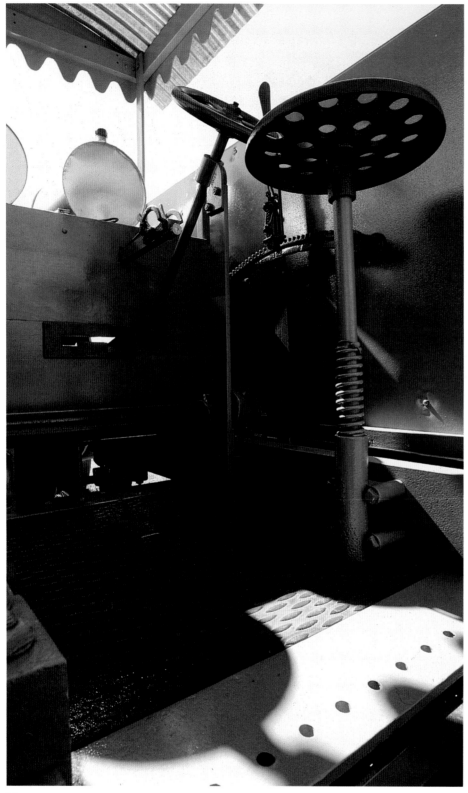

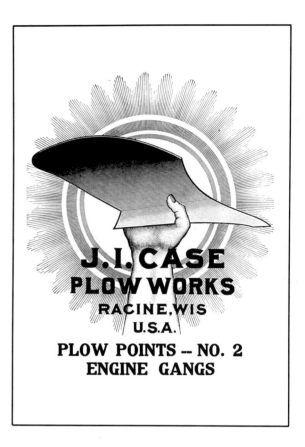

was replaced by the new 12-20 in 1922. Case advertised the 12-20 as "the best and most practical small tractor on the market."

The one-piece cast frame placed the engine, transmission and rear axle in one rigid assembly. The engine cylinder head, transmission cover and locking differential cover bolted on to provide additional rigidity yet allow for easier serviceability. The transverse-mounted engine drove through bull gears and pinions, sealed inside the frame. Dirt was eliminated, and the drive gearing was simplified. Its compact design—9 ft., 1 in. length, 24 ft. turning circle and 4,230 lb. weight—would still pull three 14 in. plows. It sold for $1,095 and, like many tractors of the day, was meant to start on gasoline and switch over to kerosene or another distillate.

As engine speeds increased and cylinder-head designs improved for better fuel and exhaust flow, tractor designations climbed. In 1925, the 15-27 grew to 18-32 and the 22-40 increased to 25-45. But the days of small, heavy and relatively expensive tractors were being numbered by Case's competitors.

The chorus of cries in the early 1920s from farm journals for a general-purpose tractor seemed to fall on deaf ears. *Agricultural Engineering* magazine, *Automotive Industries* and *Implement & Tractor* all argued that the design of the standard tractor limited it to less than half of the field work that could be mechanized. Surveys suggested that a row crop and general-purpose tractor would perform more than three fourths of the jobs. Writers criticized

manufacturers for lack of responsiveness. The post World War I depression and Ford versus IH price war may have led to a lack of resources for design and development.

Still, some just didn't listen.

Sometime in 1922, J. I. Case commissioned G. B. Gunlogson to study the market support for a new type of tractor. As Robert Williams pointed out in his history, *Fordson, Farmall and Poppin' Johnny*, Gunlogson concluded that

The 1915 Heider Model C 12–20 hp was built in Carroll, Iowa, and restored by Richard Collison and Homer Langenfeld, above and far left. Above left, the J. I. Case Plow Works had a busy career separate from the J. I. Case Threshing Machine Co.

Heider used the Waukesha four-cylinder 4.50x6.75 in. engines. The tractors were marketed by Rock Island Plow, which took over their manufacture after 1915. Far right, cross-mounted gasoline and kerosene engines were a trademark of J. I. Case from their first models through 1929. This 12–20 is part of Fred Heidrick's collection in Woodland, California.

"while the farmer and technology were ready for horseless farming, the manufacturers were not . . . . Tractor makers were tinkering and fine tuning for a limited market, when a cheaper and more versatile tractor—one that could cultivate—would open up a whole new world of sales. . . . The average farmer—the one with 160 acres and only $1,400 in equipment—would also be able to purchase a tractor."

Case chose to wait and see. Three years later, Leon Clausen became Case's president. The Deere board member who pushed production of Deere's Model D, this advocate of the all-purpose tractor was now at Case's top. The company continued producing its cross-mount

standards through the 1920s, but in 1929, it unveiled its new L, still a standard configuration but with the engine now mounted lengthwise. The L used Case's four-cylinder engine tested and developed to the highest level of efficiency. A scaled-down version, the C was introduced soon after. It was offered in orchard and industrial versions from the start.

Case had other business affairs occupying its financial resources: the other Case company, the J. I. Case Plow Works, owned Wallis Tractors. In 1928, the Case Plow Works was sold to Massey-Harris in Canada, which needed the tractors and the plows but not the Case name. J. I. Case Threshing Machine Company bought

The 12–20 replaced Case's earlier tricycle 10–20. The rage for tricycles ended when farmers experienced roll-overs. Despite the additional wheel, the new 12–20 weighed nearly 800 lb. less than its predecessor.

the name back for $700,000. The sale ended many years of confusion over the two separate companies founded by the same man, in business with similar names.

Case also bought Emerson-Brantingham, a Rockford, Illinois, tractor and implement company.

Nearly a decade later, in 1937, Case purchased a fifty-five-year-old Illinois plow and implements company, Rock Island Plow Company, to acquire its full line of tillage and harvesting equipment. Rock Island Plow was originally founded in 1855. It came to an agreement with Heider Manufacturing of Carroll, Iowa, to market its tractor. Heider's friction-drive trac-

tors resembled the earliest Case friction tractors; the entire engine moved forwards or backwards to engage drive and increase speed. Heider's own engine was a four-cylinder.

Rock Island Plow met great success selling these machines. Heider, which had already expanded its factory to meet increased demand, found that by 1914, it could not keep up. With other interests pressing, the Heiders sold their tractor business to Rock Island Plow in 1916. The plow company continued manufacturing Heider tractors until 1927.

In 1932, Case brought out its CC, the row crop version, advertising it as "2 tractors in 1" and boasting adjustable rear wheel spacing from 48 to 84 inches, power lift to raise and lower the implements, independent rear wheel brakes and a 5.1 mph top speed. PTO was optional, as was a standard front wheel axle.

In 1935, Case introduced its "motor-lift," which raised implements on the fly with the touch of a button. In addition, a simplified mounting system for its new implements made equipment change much faster. By this time, Case was offering its all-purpose tractor on rubber.

The R Series was introduced in 1936, using a Waukesha four. Available until 1940, it was offered in standard, all-purpose and industrial configurations. With the R tractors, styling arrived at Case. Its new radiator grilles reflected a spray of wheat.

The most stunning introduction came in 1939 with the new Model D, shown under spotlights to dealers at the Racine head office. Gone was the gray paint scheme that nearly twenty years earlier had replaced the cross-motors' green. Flambeau Red joined the palette of other colors working US farm fields. Flambeau, the French word for "torch," was also the name of a Wisconsin river.

Harking back to the adoption of its eagle

Tested at the University of Nebraska in August 1922, the 12–20 powered by kerosene produced 13.15 drawbar hp.

Pulling 1,703 lb. at 2.9 mph, the 12–20 was just shy of its top speed.

mascot from a Wisconsin Civil War regiment, Case also introduced Eagle-Eye visibility, the result of a higher, fully adjustable operator seat and more vertical steering wheel. The D used Case's four-cylinder engine with the four-speed transmission in the DC row crop, good for 10 mph on the roads.

The next year, Case replaced the R with its new V in all versions. A two-plow-rated S Series came out as well. The VA replaced the V in 1942, and Case's first high-crop tractor, the VAH, was introduced. The company continued the S and VA Series as well as the D in production until 1955.

Old Abe adorns the radiator of the Case 12–20. Introduced in 1922, the 12–20 was produced until 1928. Below, the Case-designed cross-mounted four cylinder was 4.125x5.00 in. bore and stroke. The belt pulley was driven by the crankshaft off the other end of the engine. Below left, a cross-mount Case tractor at work powering a belt-driven thresher on Jim Keenan's Flandreau, South Dakota, farm in 1930.

POWER!

PLENTY OF IT AND AT THE LEAST EXPENSE

THE 60 H.P. OIL TRACTOR BURNS GASOLINE, NAPTHA DISTILLATE ETC.

40 H.P. GASOLINE TRACTOR BURNS GASOLINE ONLY

That's what you'll get when you invest in a

CASE GAS OR OIL TRACTOR

SEE THEM AT THE FAIRS OR AT NEAREST BRANCH HOUSE

Have Them Demonstrated

J.I.CASE THRESHING MACHINE CO.

INCORPORATED

RACINE, WIS. U.S.A.

In 1953, Case changed its nomenclature and colors and added diesel power. The 500 Series six-cylinder diesel produced 56 hp and came standard with dual disc brakes, electric

Case's 60 hp and 40 hp were two of the best machines of their days. By 1948, the Case LA was the top of the line, far left.

89

By the early 1950s, Case LAs were available with gasoline, distillate and LPG engines. Gasoline proved the most powerful, pulling 3,347 lb., nearly 70 lb. more than LPG and 580 lb. more than the distillate-fuel version. Right, fitted with 7.50x18 in. pneumatic tires at front and 15x30 in. rears, the Case LA weighed 7,621 lb. The hand crank easily turned over the big Case four-cylinder engine. Far right, Case's own four-cylinder on the Model LA had 4.625x6.00 in. bore and stroke. Overall displacement was 403 ci. In fourth gear, the tractor was capable of slightly more than 10 mph.

lights and starter. The 400 Series arrived in 1955, and the 300s arrived in 1956. With the introduction of the 500s, Case tractors adopted two-tone paint, Flambeau Red with Desert Sand.

The new numbered series featured Powr-Torq engines, which ran on gas, LPG, distillates or diesel. The Tripl-Range twelve-speed transmission offered 12 mph in road gear. And Case's Eagle Hitch three-point implement hookup monitored plow depth and increased traction. The 300s rated three plows, the 400s rated four plows and in 1957, a new 600 Series offered six speeds and a six-plow rating. In 1958, Case introduced its 700, 800 and 900 Series tractors and, with them, the Case-O-Matic transmissions. The 900 diesels with their 4x5 in. 377 ci six-cylinder engines rated 70 hp.

In 1957, Case entered the crawler market by purchasing American Tractor Company of Chu-

rubusco, Indiana, makers since 1950 of the Terratrac. An innovative company, American Tractor offered GT–25 and GT–30 gasoline and DT–34 diesel models with interchangeable track gauges for row-crop applications, a three-point hydraulic hitch and track shoes of either steel or rubber. Through the 1950s, Case continued Terratrac production at Churubusco.

In 1967, Case was purchased by Kern County Land Co., which was soon purchased itself by Tenneco, a Houston, Texas, conglomerate founded on oil. Two years later, the Case eagle, Old Abe, retired. In 1972, Case acquired David Brown Tractors, of England.

In the next ten years, the economy, having expanded with a boomtown mentality during the previous ten years, began shrinking from the effects of war in Vietnam and from industrial over-production. Power farming suffered from

the muscle flexing of Middle East oil-producing nations. Gasoline and diesel fuel prices multiplied while food prices dropped.

In 1984, Tenneco took over International Harvester's farm tractor and implement division, substantially strengthening is position in the tractor market. Yet within three years, Tenneco considered selling Case because that division's losses were so serious. The addition of International Harvester made the situation acute. But in 1988, Tenneco decided instead to sell all its oil holdings. As Tenneco restructured, its largest division was Case-IH.

Chapter 6

International Harvester

*Ford had convinced thousands of horse-using farmers that in
the tractor they could find the answer to their power needs.
International proved to them that to do their work they must
have a superior machine. . . . There can be no such thing as a
good cheap tractor.*
Cyrus McCormick III, The Century of the Reaper, 1931

International Harvester's tractor division was born of decades of manufacturing other implements, leading to the realization that this new machine was a necessary adjunct to the catalog.

On July 25, 1831, Cyrus Hall McCormick was an inventive twenty-two year old, born of fourth-generation Scotch-Irish immigrants. The family farm in Walnut Grove, Virginia (a town too small now to register on a map) was prosperous, including substantial acreage, gristmills, saw-mills, a smelter and a blacksmith shop. Cyrus' father, Robert, was a dreamer and tireless inventor and for the first seven years of Cyrus' life had tried to build himself a mechanical reaper. His utter failures in the past and over the next fifteen years had discouraged him but put a challenge to Cyrus. Ignorant of failures elsewhere in the world, Cyrus continued to dream his father's dream with the freshness and enthusiasm of youth.

So, independent of the inventors who had come before, Cyrus McCormick slowly accumulated all the principles necessary and created a reaper. But he wasn't satisfied with his first effort, even though farmers around Walnut Grove were excited. He nudged it, modified it, corrected it and in 1834 patented it, still realizing that it was not yet perfect.

The family's investments turned sour, and still McCormick fidgeted with the reaper. The family's fortunes diminished and returned, and still McCormick modified and improved until in 1840, he sold his first, and his second.

In 1841, McCormick returned to work, since his first two reapers were not successes. He changed the cutting angle of the knives, and with recognition building, he sold seven machines in 1842.

Seven sold in 1842 led to twenty-nine sold in 1843 and to fifty sold in 1844. Word spread through newspaper accounts; inquiries came to Walnut Grove, and McCormick's small factory—in fact, a family shed—was strained to capacity. McCormick traveled to promote the tractor and to find other shops to manufacture it. When

Logo of IHC, pride of Canada in 1914. Left, Raymond Pollock of Denison, Iowa, bought his 1939 McCormick Deering F20 after losing three of his horses to lightning in 1948. He has used it nearly every day since.

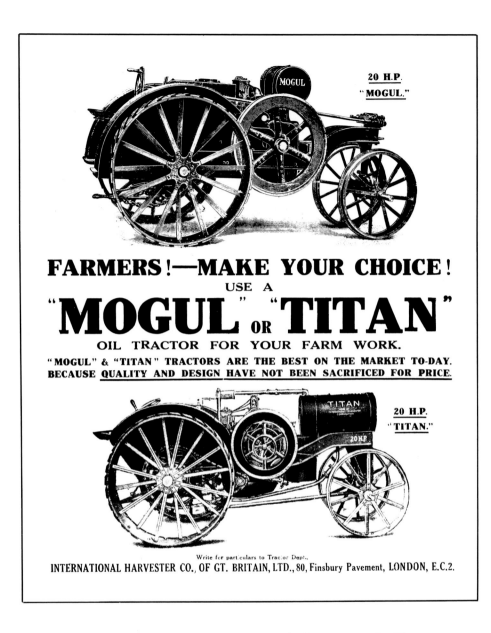

An English ad for the International Mogul and Titan, two of the best tractors available in the 1910s. These two 20 hp kerosene-burning models were highly developed and downsized versions of the original prairie giants.

shipping each $100 reaper to the West meant an additional $25 in freight, McCormick thought of shipping the factory west. He looked to Chicago. In 1847, after 1846 sales of 123 machines, he moved.

The history of any innovative inventor-designer-manufacturer is filled with patent disputes. McCormick's initial protection in 1834 was to be renewed in 1948. Yet the patent board refused, judging his reaper too valuable to remain in private control. The license agreements with several firms became royalty free, but in

their freedom they still lacked McCormick himself. He continued to modify and improve the machines. When the licenses expired, he did not renew; when partnerships frayed, he bought back his independence.

As the discovery of gold in California removed thousands of farmers and helpers from the East and Midwest, the market for his reapers expanded. The food requirements of a huge population now located in the Far West, no longer engaged in food production, meant top prices for the Midwest farmers. And those profits meant new machines.

Some similarity exists between the industrial lives of Cyrus McCormick and John Deere. Both men moved to the West (meaning Illinois in those days) in search of broader opportunities. Throughout their lives, they devoted their efforts to the perfection of one tool and in so doing virtually defined the machine for all time. From Deere came the shape of the plow still used more than 150 years later. From McCormick came the principles that still govern the success of any harvester today. With Deere and McCormick, the achievement of perfection of their one implement meant success in staggering numbers. Both men, conservative and proud, resisted stubbornly the encroachment of the next-generation improvements. And with each, it was left to their heirs and successors to take over and to experiment with diversification.

McCormick's next decade was most trying, beginning with the lantern kicked over by Mrs. Patrick O'Leary's cow on Chicago's North Side. By the time the embers cooled, the Chicago fire of 1871 had destroyed more than 15,000 buildings and $180 million in property over 3½ square miles and had left 94,000 homeless.

McCormick's age gave him brief pause. He was sixty-two and tremendously wealthy. Yet retirement was never considered. Instead he rebuilt. And once more he found himself in the fray.

The new challenge came from a former dry goods merchant, another New England refugee who arrived in Chicago in 1873, William Deering. His efforts shook McCormick's primacy.

McCormick had lost the competitive edge when he refused to adapt to newer technology.

The pace of the recent years proved too much, and McCormick died in 1884. Within months, the legacy coalesced into the first organized labor confrontations, and to riots at

Haymarket Square. But McCormick's son Cyrus had already spent five years as his father's secretary, and at twenty-five, though young, he took over the worldwide industrial corporation.

Through the next six years, McCormick battled Deering and his other competitors for the market. From time to time, talk of a merger surfaced. In 1897 the Deerings offered their company to young McCormick. The Deerings were older and ready to surrender in order to retire comfortably. But McCormick was too far

extended keeping ahead of the Deerings while continuing expansion in the European market. For the Deerings, the problems were similar; expanding production to challenge McCormick had strained their finances as well.

The Deerings had begun acquiring their own suppliers. By 1902, Deering was much more self-sufficient, and the manufacturing took on a new efficiency. McCormick's strength was in his enormous, resourceful outside sales staff. McCormick knew that continuing against Deering

Looking more like an early sports car gone off course, the 1918 International 8–16 drew some design inspiration from automobile styles of the period.

95

Power for the 8–16 came from International's four-cylinder valve-in-head 4x5 in. engine. Its sleek shape placed the radiator at the farmer's feet, which made summer work particularly unpleasant. Below, the 8–16s were fitted with carburetors capable of handling kerosene or gasoline fuel. An experimental crawler was produced this same year but did not see regular production.

meant gaining similar self-sufficiency—and that meant money. So, in June 1902, McCormick went to the bankers to secure financing.

George Perkins, the youngest partner in J. P. Morgan, listened intently. By late July, Perkins succeeded in convincing several manufacturers of the advantages of consolidation.

Competition during the past decade had led to overproduction and overpopulation. With each manufacturer hustling for every sale, the firms' stock on hand far exceeded realistic sales expectations. Whenever a competitor opened a sales branch in one locale, the others opened there as well. By 1902, more than 40,000 dealers were in existence.

Cyrus McCormick III, grandson of McCormick's founder and author of *The Century of the Reaper*, understood that the amalgamation would eliminate duplication and allow the strengths of each organization to be exploited to the best advantage.

"The future profits of the Harvester Company were to come," Cyrus McCormick III reflected, "not from any expansion of the 'old lines', but from the business to be built up in later years in other lines of agricultural implements and in lines of trade that were not even dreamed of in the early part of the twentieth century."

So Perkins swung the deal. On August 12, 1902, $60 million changed hands. The International Harvester Company acquired the factories, warehouses, inventories and properties of Milwaukee Harvester, Plano Harvester, Champion Reaper, Marsh Harvester, Deering Harvester and McCormick Harvesting Machinery Company.

Cyrus McCormick was the new president; Charles Deering, William's son, was chairman of the board of directors.

Then in 1906, in Upper Sandusky, Ohio, the new conglomerate produced its first tractors.

Cyrus McCormick III observed that "a tractor is purposeless if it is not able to work at all times under maximum stresses and strains. An automobile does not have to run at top speed for every minute of its productive life, an airplane engine is always in the hands of the most skilled mechanics to check or repair an incipient ill. The tractor has to work—it has to be designed for never ending toil, for the task of furnishing available, immediate, and dependable farm power."

Cyrus McCormick's grandson benefited from twenty-five years of hindsight: "The social importance of the reaper was that it substituted horse-power for the tired muscles of straining peasants; the social importance of the tractor is that it substitutes mechanical power for those tasks which sap the strength of men and animals. Both brought the power of machinery to the aid of man.... Progressively, they freed men's minds from the apparent delusion of necessity: and then presented an opportunity for work with brains as a better substitute for work with brawn."

International Harvester's first tractors used the Milwaukee-built horizontal 15 hp one-cylinder Famous engine mounted on a frame made by Morton Manufacturing of Upper Sandusky. The engine was mounted on rollers on the frame and shifted forwards or backwards to engage friction drive. In 1906, IH produced twenty-five of these for testing and development. The results were good, so in 1907, an additional 200 were produced. The Morton Traction friction drive eventually proved unsuitable, and when tractor

International 8–16s were produced at the Chicago plant. Introduced in 1917, the kerosene burner remained in production through 1922. Below, a three-speed transmission offered a top speed of 4 mph, not exactly in keeping with the tractor's race-car looks. Total production for its five-year life was 33,138.

Joan Hollenitsch of Garden Grove, California, owns this 8–16 kerosene. She keeps it and runs it at the Antique Gas and Steam Engine Museum at Vista, California, near San Diego. Below, the Farmall general-purpose tractor was introduced in 1924, and set the basic design for the row-crop tractors still in use today. This McCormick-Deering Farmall F-12 was the smallest of the series, developing 2¼ to 3½ hp, ideal for the small farmer.

production was transferred to the former Aultman-Miller works in Akron, geared transmissions were used.

The company introduced the Type A, offered between 1907 and 1911 and available in 12 hp, 15 hp or 20 hp rating. A 20 hp Type B was introduced in 1908, the only difference being a split rear axle. Friction drive was retained only for reverse, but by 1910, gears completely replaced the Morton system.

International Harvester, like many companies before and after, attempted to maintain separate lines of production for each of its former independents. Between 1909 and 1914, it produced the Mogul for sale by McCormick dealers. The 20 hp machines were heavy but reliable. For Deering distributors, the company introduced the Titan, rated at 27–45 hp in 1910, and increased it to 30–60 hp before 1915. International Harvester's goal of equal products for separate divisions was tripped up. The designers of the Mogul profited from their experiences before undertaking the Titan.

The Winnipeg trials were inaugurated in 1908. Of ten manufacturers competing, IH came second. The Canadian market was large and influential, and a good performance there guaranteed sales. But the Canadian demand was for ever-larger prairie-sodbusting monsters. Horsepower escalated until in the 1912 exhibitions, IH linked three Titans together, pulled fifty-five plows and turned a swath 64 ft. wide.

Meanwhile, writers for US farm magazines and newspapers called repeatedly for smaller machines. The giants were too expensive and too hard to maintain. The average farmer, accustomed to moderately priced implements, had little mechanical experience.

In 1913, outside competition provoked IH to reconsider size. D. M. Hartsough's Little Bull was introduced as a $395 tricycle tractor. Although it lacked power to work the fields, it had enough power to draw interest. IH took note.

The next year, its kerosene-fired single-cylinder Mogul 8-16 was introduced. This was followed in 1915 by the twin-cylinder Titan 10-20. The economic timing of these introductions was serendipitous—the economy in the United States was improving, and the threat of war in Europe created an additional market for food and fiber. The wisdom of this direction change was proven by sales numbers: between 1907 and 1917, IH sold about 13,750 of the large A, B, C and D Moguls and Titans. From the 1914 introduction to the end of 1917, it sold 14,065 of the Moguls, and between 1915 and 1922, it sold another 78,000 of the Titan 10-20s.

As the tractor market settled, International Harvester faced reorganization. Following an antitrust suit, a federal court order forced sale of the Osborne, Champion and Milwaukee implement companies.

The same suit charged IH with maintaining dual dealerships in areas where both McCormick and Deering outlets still existed. Eight thousand dealers were let go by 1919. The parallel products were combined, hybridizing what was believed best in each. The new line was called McCormick-Deering. The remaining 13,800 dealers broadened their bases, each carrying the full line of McCormick *and* Deering implements.

International Harvester was left leaner and more streamlined as it entered the 1920s. The American farmer was undeniably ready for a leaner, smaller tractor. Whether International Harvester was ready for Henry Ford was another question altogether.

Tractors in 1910 averaged 504 lb. per horsepower. That year, IH took the tractor production lead, ahead of Rumely and Hart-Parr.

In 1915, Henry Ford announced his small, lightweight tractor, and most of the eighty other companies in business at the time went on largely unconcerned. The same year, Philip Rose examined Ford in his *Black Book,* but he never saw a production Fordson. His assessment of the Ford tractor models he saw led him to dismiss the effort as inconsequential: "The machine as it stands at the present time is not a farm tractor. The only features of the machine which appeal to me are the compactness and nimbleness of the outfit.

But Rose was, in the end, misled: "Personally I do not think that tractor manufacturers need to worry regarding the present Ford outfit. If he could go into the tractor business he will learn in a very short time that the present outfit will not stand up."

In 1917, Ford shipped 7,000 Fordsons to the United Kingdom. The same year, the Society of Automotive Engineers joined the Society of Tractor Engineers. Implement companies gained access almost overnight to information never before available to the engineers who had to design tractors.

International Harvester's 1918 International 8-16 weighed 3,300 lb., or 206 lb. per horsepower. Ford's 1918 Fordson weighed 2,700 lb., or 150 lb. per horsepower.

In 1918, with war in Europe and 7,000 sales in the United Kingdom, Ford attacked the home front. The war subsequently involved American farmers, and an anticipated reduction in tractor demand became an increase. The Fordson passed IH's tractors in production. In 1920, when total production from all makers hit 203,000, Ford was producing several times as many as International Harvester and nearly three fourths of the total. By this time, Cyrus McCormick III was an integral part of the operations, and his recollections are immediate: "Sales fell off to a quarter, inventories of materials and unsold tractors were huge and high-priced and prospects were gloomy. Then, early in 1922, Henry Ford cut the price of tractors.

"That February morning is another of the many business hours I treasure in my memory. I had taken Mr. [Alexander] Legge, the Company's beloved and hard-boiled general manager, on a visit to the new motor-truck installation at Springfield works. As we were arguing some problem which then seemed to be important, the telephone rang—Chicago wished to speak to Mr. Legge. We could, of course hear only his side of the conversation. There was much talk from the other end, and then an explosion from Alex: 'What? What's that? How much? Two hundred and thirty dollars? Well, I'll be . . . What'll we do about it? Do? Why damn it all—meet him, of course! We're going to stay in the tractor business. Yes, cut two hundred and thirty dollars. Both models—yes, both. And say, listen, make it good! We'll throw in a plow as well.'"

Ford's timing was impeccable. His price cut—and Legge's life-and-death response—came on the eve of the 1922 National Tractor Show in Minneapolis. The show served as the death notice for dozens of manufacturers who couldn't meet Ford's price and remain in business, but who would sell no more tractors if they didn't meet Ford's price.

That often-repeated story takes on greater significance with McCormick's own interpretation. "Harvester was waging the battle of the implement industry against mighty Henry Ford and the automobile," he began. "Ford was backed by the most popular commercial name of the time and the uncounted millions earned for him by his epoch-making car. . . . Doubtless Ford had no overt desire to attack Harvester; as he said later, he was simply trying to find out how low the price might be at which farmers would buy tractors in quantities equivalent to automobiles."

International Harvester did fight back, cutting the price of the Titan 10–20 to $700 and the price of the International 8–16 to $670. That included its Parlin & Orendorf derived number 5 Little Genius plow. It quickly consumed the tractor stock piles. Still, with the Fordson at $395, the advantage lay with Ford. And worse, the price wars meant both companies were selling below cost; some outside suppliers charged more than $395 just for their engines. For IH, without the automobile revenues Ford enjoyed, production costs had to be trimmed in ways never before imagined.

International Harvester's salespeople turned every Fordson demonstration into a field contest, and its tractors won each time a competition was run. By the end of 1924, IH sales increased. By 1927, McCormick-Deering agricultural tractors outsold Fordsons as more and

A McCormick-Deering W–30 Farmall standard-tread at work. The W–30 series was constructed during the 1932–1940 period, and was developed into the W–4.

Raymond Pollock's F20 is a working machine, not a tractor-show antique. Pollock is still impressed with it. His only repairs amounted to twice having the valves reground. The International four has 3.75x5.00 bore and stroke. Pollock's German Shepard, Reggie, knows the value of a good tractor in the shade it casts. Below, Pollock remembered the difference between his horses and his tractor: twelve acres a day with horses was hard work; twenty acres a day, plowed and harrowed, with the Farmall was easier.

more farmers realized the work they needed to perform could be better accomplished with International Harvesters. And in 1928, when Fordson's industrial tractor production slipped as well, the combination of circumstances led Ford to end tractor production.

Still, from the nearly fatal tractor wars came some corporate benefit. McCormick recognized the value. "It is questionable if the business of making tractors would so soon have become a large-scale industry had it not been for Ford," he reflected in 1931 when he wrote *The Century of the Reaper.* "In 1918, the manufacturing methods employed by all tractor producers were derived from implement and not automotive standards. . . . The record annual production of 4,000 Mogul 8-16's in 1915 had been non-progressively assembled; at a period in its early existence the flywheel of a Titan 10–20 traveled exactly one mile around the factory (as compared with a subsequent 300 feet) before it was mounted in the tractor."

When IH replaced the International 8–16 in 1922, more than 33,000 had been sold. Introduced first at $1,150, the tractor finally sold for

Introduced in 1932, the F20 replaced International Harvester's Farmall Regular. By 1935, the F20 was sold on pneumatic rubber tires, for about $2,000.

Akron just to keep up with orders. But McCormick wanted his own.

Johnston began in Akron, but the Tractor Works came home to Chicago in 1909 when his Mogul took off. Sometime the next year, Alexander Legge met with him to discuss the idea of a smaller, general-purpose tractor. International Harvester's Motor Cultivator was born, adding new patents to Johnston's list and a new title to his name: Experimental Division manager. Johnston and a persistent experimenter among his crew, Bert Benjamin, continued refining the new tractor. But management continued promoting and selling the McCormick-Deering line with such success that little encouragement existed to replace a proven moneymaker.

That is, until Ford's tractor knocked IH far out of its comfortable first place. Barbara Marsh, in her book *A Corporate Tragedy — The Agony of International Harvester Company*, related the turning point in the Farmall tractor's history: In July 1921 "Legge called a meeting of his top executives. Legge outlined Henry Ford's brisk takeover of the market and his rapid advance into tractor attachments and demanded to know what had ever happened to the ten experimental Farmall tractors in the engineering department. Edward Johnston quickly rose to his own defense and claimed he'd received little management encouragement to develop the new tractors and associated attachments. Johnston insisted, however, that the Farmall was superior to the Fordson and exemplified the future of power farming."

Legge, progressive but patient, gave Johnston the encouragement to develop a machine that would replace all the animal power on a farm. Benjamin had been working on a cultivator, configured as a reversed tricycle, with its driving wheel also doing the steering at the rear. But the cultivator wouldn't draw a sod-breaker plow through unbroken prairie. So Benjamin reversed the whole affair, moving the engine to about the middle of the channel-iron frame. The rear end—the former front end—would straddle two rows. A high rear-axle clearance was meant to clear early growth corn or cotton or to allow room for the cultivator to be hung below the engine. The front end, slipping between the rows, was tied by linkage to the leading cultivator shovels, so that when the farmer steered away from corn or cotton crops, the shovels led away too.

less than half that, including the value of the free two-bottom plow. Its replacement broke new ground in many ways: it was International Harvester's first unit frame tractor, strengthening and lightening the tractor greatly. The Milwaukee Works-produced tractor used International Harvester's own 4.5x6 in. four-cylinder engine. Rear power take-off was introduced to farmers as an option on the model known as the Gear Drive 15–30. More than 99,800 were produced by 1929, when The New 15–30 was introduced.

In 1923, as IH fought Ford, its engineers tested the first general-purpose tractors. The Fordson's failures—low ground clearance that precluded its use in corn and cotton crops after planting, and wheel placement that required too much maneuvering room—were targets for IH engineers.

E dward A. Johnston joined International Harvester before the turn of the century. He earned the first of his eventual 171 patents at IH in 1897 when he was twenty-two. By 1907, Johnston had produced International Harvester's first farm truck, a huge success. Cyrus McCormick then asked Johnston to develop a new tractor. The Morton machine was selling well, and McCormick built a new factory in

Another twenty Farmall prototypes were ordered built, along with every conceivable implement—all by hand. Testing was to go on until absolutely no bugs remained. More patents came to Johnston and his staff, and the first production Farmall was sold in Iowa in 1924.

Millions of dollars were spent. Dealer follow-up was the highest priority, and several successful ideas resulted from farmers' own adaptations of the new International Harvester machine. The aggressive and costly sales techniques paid off in the end, when in 1928, Ford threw in the towel and IH resumed the lead in tractor production.

C. H. Wendel, in his *150 Years of International Harvester*, researched in incredible detail the variety of machines IH offered. The first Farmall had no model designation, and International Harvester executives resisted the temptation to label it with horsepower ratings. The first 200 examples, which were hand-built preproduction models, sold for $825, but a year later in regular production, the price was set at $950; fenders were an extra $15. The tractor was powered by International Harvester's four-cylinder engine, which produced 9-18 hp at 1200 rpm. Production increased like untended weeds: from 200 in 1924 to 838 in 1925 to 4,430 in 1926 and to 9,502 in 1927. By the end of January 1930, the Tractor Works was turning out 200 machines per day, and from February 20, 1924, when production was authorized, to April 12, 1930, 100,000 Farmalls were built.

In 1930, the first Farmall adopted a name, the Regular, when a new version, the F-30, was introduced. Production of the F-30 didn't approach the Regular's numbers, but in 1932, IH introduced a companion F-20 model, using the Regular's engine. At 1200 rpm, the F-20 produced 20 drawbar hp. Available on rubber in 1935, it sold for $1,050, and throughout its eight-year life, it sold well: 148,960 copies. It was essentially a slightly larger, slightly more powerful Regular.

A corresponding standard-tread version of the F-30 was McCormick-Deering's W-30 but with slightly increased power—19-31 hp. On rubber in 1935, it sold for $1,135, $85 more than its row crop cousin. Orchard versions were available. In total, more than 32,000 W-30s were sold through 1940.

The F-12 was introduced in 1932, selling more than 123,000 by its end in 1938. The F-12

rated 12-16 hp, weighed not quite 3,000 lb. and sold for $797.50. In 1934, a W-12 was offered, following the W-30 series.

From the start of the Farmall series, a full range of Farmall-compatible implements was available. A rapid mounting system, called Quick Attach, meant that changeover took minutes. Everything from golf course fairway lawn mower gangs to plows and cultivators was offered.

International Harvester's F-14 was offered only in 1938 and 1939. Fewer than 28,000 examples of this interim model were sold. On rubber, a row crop F-14 sold for $895. A small run of W-14 tractors was produced, at $785 on rubber.

A big tractor, the W-40, was introduced in 1934. Using a six-cylinder, the W-40 generated 35-50 hp. More important, the diesel version in 1934, the WD-40, was the first US-built wheel-tractor to use Rudolf Diesel's engine. It pro-

International Harvester was producing crawlers with diesels by 1936. This 1941 Model TD-14 also featured Raymond Loewy's stylish sheet metal. This crawler is part of the collection at the Antique Gas and Steam Engine Museum, Vista, California.

The TD–14 was powered by International's 4.75x6.50 in. four cylinder. In Nebraska tests, the TD–14 rated 61.56 brake hp and towed 13,426 lb. Below, the TD–14 was introduced in 1939. More than 26,250 were sold during its ten-year life. It weighed 17,595 lb. and in sixth gear could reach 5.75 mph.

duced 37-49 hp. On rubber, the WD-40 sold for $2,516, powered by International Harvester's own four-cylinder. It was started as a gasoline engine, hand cranked, and then the engine automatically switched over to diesel fuel.

As early as 1926, IH experimented with crawler versions of the McCormick-Deering 15-30. More work went on based on the 10-20, and a crawler, called the TracTracTor, entered regular production in 1929. Fitted with steering clutches, it was basically a wheel-type 10-20 and 15-30 chassis adapted for tracks. The 10-20 weighed in at 7,250 lb., and only 1,505 units were produced during its two-year life.

The TracTracTor T-20 became the working model for IH crawlers. By the end of production in 1939, more than 15,000 had been manufactured. Foot brakes supplemented the steering clutches; square corner turns were now possible. An orchard version, offered in the 10-20, was continued with the T-20. The T-20 sold for $1,495, and for an additional $70, a wide tread

Raymond Pollock:

The Farmer's Holiday of the 1930s

"You hear about the new tractor? It's got no seat and no steering wheel. That's for the farmer that has lost his ass and doesn't know which way to turn!"

Raymond Pollock loves a good joke, especially a good farmer joke. Farming all his life in western Iowa, he has had experiences that mirror those of thousands of others, and he has seen enough difficulty to appreciate a finely told tale.

"Fellow in town won the lottery the other night. They had him on the TV and asked him what he was going to do. He said—Well, I'm gonna take this million dollars and farm till I go broke."

Pollock knows about going broke, too. He hasn't, but he knows it hasn't been easy.

"I could have bought 200 acres of land one time for $6,000, $30 an acre. And you couldn't borrow fifteen cents. Back in the thirties they called it the Farm Holiday. It was a bunch of farmers got together. They were foreclosing on all the farmers and selling them out and putting them out on the road. I knew of an instance up northeast of here. They served notice on a farmer and put him and his family out on the road. And they slept *on* the road for two days and two nights. They had no place to go. There was no relief in those days. There was nothing."

Pollock's voice trails off. It not only seems so long ago, it seems almost like another life. These were the horrible hard experiences from your youth that framed the rest of your life, that developed the perspectives that showed you the truth. This was the war in your own backyard.

"And then down here west of Denison, they had this riot. This guy had rented the farm for, I think, $10 an acre. Well it came up there in the fall. Stuff wasn't worth anything. Hogs were three cents a pound, corn was a dime a bushel. He offered the landlord all the crop that he raised plus all the hogs and calves. The guy wouldn't take it, so he ordered a foreclosure.

"The Farm Holiday stepped in. 'No you ain't gonna sell this land out! He's too good a fellah!'

"The farmers were desperate. They were broke. They came up there to that sale in a great big truck, just like cattle. They had a twenty-foot bed on it and it was just clear full of farmers. They were all carrying clubs, maul handles, axe handles.

"Well, they started the sale. A guy bid ten cents on a cow, you know, was all he bid. So the sheriff stopped the sale.

"And they started to fight.

"And I'll tell you what. They clubbed the authorities till the blood was running. . . . I was there! I *saw* it.

"And one guy pulled a gun on a bunch of farmers, see. They grabbed his gun. There was a tank full of water and they said to the guy 'What are you running this water tank for?' and he said 'Well, I might have to cool some of you farmers down.' And they threw him in there and damned near drowned the demon. It was in February, in the cold weather."

Pollock laughs again at what seems like a prank half a century later. At the time, it was not. His eyes sparkle now inside his strong, wiry seventy-five-year-old body. There is pride in the accomplishment of simply living through those days.

"I farmed with horses. That F–20 was quite an improvement. You see by the time you harness up five horses, it takes you quite a while and you gotta bring them in at noon, unhitch 'em, feed 'em and water 'em. Then you go back and when you come back in at night, it's the same old thing over again. It's quite a bit of work. Of course, I always had outlaws too. I didn't have good horses. Kick your head off or run away from you.

"That Farmall was the first tractor I ever bought. See the only reason I even bought that tractor was because I lost those horses to lightning. Otherwise I wasn't in any hurry to get a tractor.

"You see, we could do ten, maybe twelve acres in a day. Even coming in for supper. 'Course, that's moving right along.

"But with a hired man, with the F–20 we plowed all eighty acres in four days, pulling two sixteens. Then harrowed it. All within four days!"

Pollock feels pride for the fifty-two-year-old tractor.

"I've never bought a new tractor, never owned a new tractor. I bought that F–20 out there in 1948. It was a 1939 model and all I've ever done to it was grind the valves a few years back. You don't need all this high-priced stuff. There's no advantage.

"What other business is there in the world where you sell everything you make for wholesale and you buy everything you need for retail?"

The 1955 International Harvester W450 gas series was powered by IHC's 4.125x5.250 in. four cylinder. Its owner, Norbert Schwabenlander of St. John, Wisconsin, bought it in 1955 with 165 hours on the clock. Below, with his brother, Schwabenlander raises oats and corn. He believes the W450 a good worker, using three gallons an hour to pull his Oliver three-bottom plow. The tractor now has more than 19,350 hours on it.

version was available. A further $300 put rubber tracks on the T-20.

For three years, from 1936 through 1939, a six-cylinder T-35 was offered. Only 499 were sold. Its wide-tread version sold for $2,415. A diesel TD-35 sold for an additional $385; it rated 36-44 hp. Full enclosure for the engine was available.

The T-40, produced from 1932 to 1939, corresponded to the W-40. The enclosed engine was now standard, and for $70, an enclosed cab was available. On wide treads, the T-40 sold for $2,850, the TD-40 for $3,600. The gas version six produced 44-52 hp. Although the diesel rated 10 hp less in drawbar power, in practical tests it pulled almost 1,000 lb. more in weight, with the additional advantages of less-expensive fuel.

To bring styling to its tractors in the 1930s, IH engaged Raymond Loewy to clean up design and appearances of its machinery, its dealerships and even the corporate logo. In his 1979 book *Industrial Design*, Loewy remembered the logo: "In view of the power and prestige of International Harvester, I thought their trademark was frail and amateurish. The firm's executives asked me to show them what I had in mind. I left Chicago for New York on the train and sketched a design on the dining-car menu, and before we passed through Fort Wayne, International Harvester had a new trademark. It was reminiscent of the front end of a tractor and its operator."

When the new crawlers were introduced in late 1938, they had all benefited from Loewy's scrutiny and imagination. The new TD-18, the T-6 and TD-6, and the TD-9 all looked newer and worked better. Loewy raised exhaust pipes to clear the operators' head, moved pedals and levers for more convenient reach, and styled a distinctive radiator grille, which also carried over into the Farmall series.

The TD-18 was produced until 1949, selling 19,183 copies; the T-6 and its diesel version were offered until 1956, with nearly 38,500 sold; the TD-9 also ended in 1956, with more than 58,000 sold. Crawlers continued to be a significant portion of International Harvester's tractor production. The 14 Series ran from 1939 to 1949, selling more than 26,000; an A version offered 10 more brake hp from 1949 through 1955.

The Farmall F Series was replaced during a two-year span by new A, B, H and K models. In 1939, the A was introduced as a $575 single-plow tractor. Producing 16-18 hp the A offered a streamlined hood and offset operator's seat that were evidence of Loewy's fine hand. Loewy's influence continued through the entire line-up. The B was the row-crop version of the A, weighing a mere 1,780 lb. and selling for $605. Both were sold into 1947.

The Model H was a 24-26 hp row crop. The H was supplemented by the M, a three-plow, 34-39 hp row-crop tractor. These tractors got caught in World War II rubber rationing, and prices were quoted either for steel wheels or about $200 more for rubber tires. Both the H and the M were also offered in high crop versions, and a diesel engine was introduced for the M in 1941.

The A and B were replaced in 1947 by the C; its main differences were a sturdier frame design, like that of the H and K, and adjustable rear track by sliding hubs. A Super M was introduced in 1952, and a Super H in 1953. The Super M introduced the Torque Amplifier dual-range transmission. A Super C was produced from 1951 to 1954 and offered Touch-Control hydraulics to lift implements or increase traction.

Standard-tread versions of the H were known as the W-4, which was introduced in 1940 and replaced in 1953 by the Super W-4, a tractor more streamlined in appearance. The W-4 and W-6 were also offered through World War II on steel. The W-6 was available as a diesel, the WD-6. At the top end came the W-9 Series, in gasoline or diesel and available as an industrial or even a rice-field version. The W-9s stayed in production through 1956. And a new small tractor was introduced in 1947. The Farmall Cub rated just 9 drawbar hp, good for a single 12 in. plow.

With all the manufacturers, the mid-1950s were a period of great reorganization in tractor lines. For IH, the changes and diversity of models introduced by 1960 were almost bewildering. McCormick Farmall 100s, 200s, 300s and 400s were introduced in 1954 and offered until 1956. Each was available in row-crop, standard and industrial configurations. The series formerly designated W was changed to International, with versions 100 through 400. In 1956 only, these were supplemented by a Farmall 600, a full five-plow standard for either gasoline or diesel fuel.

Late in 1956, the Farmall and International 100 and 200 Series were upgraded to 130 and 230, the 300 and 400 became 350 and 450, the giant 600 became 650, and all of them introduced a new color scheme, adding white to the grille and to hood slashes. This series change was produced only until 1958, when a major restyling took place in addition to model designation changes yet again.

In 1958, the grille was substantially redesigned, to give a much more aggressive, forceful appearance. The bottom models were now 140 and 240; the 350s were replaced by 330 and 340 models; the 450s became 460s; 560s were introduced as five-plow tractors, to supplement the new 660s. In all series above 240, gasoline, diesel or LPG engines could be ordered. Virtually the entire line-up in 1958, 1959 and 1960 was offered in standard-front, row-crop or single-front-wheel configurations.

The decades of the 1960s and 1970s brought the best of times and the worst of times to the United States and to International Harvester. By 1979, IH had lost the lead in tractor sales to Deere and all tractor sales had lost out to tight money. Personnel changes in IH management brought some unrealistic production goals and on November 1, 1979, the United Automobile Workers (UAW) struck International Harvester.

Five and a half months later the strike was settled and six months after that, the US Federal Reserve Bank raised the prime lending rate to 21.5 percent. Bank financing dried up and tractor sales all but ceased. The strike had cost IH $540 million within a year and had taken its credit rating from the highest to the lowest.

Then in 1982 IH got serious. It sold its construction equipment division, closed factories, consolidated other operations, laid off thousands of long-time employees. And it lost $1.7 billion.

Then at last, ten years and three and a half weeks after the UAW struck International Harvester, the company surrendered its heritage. Tenneco, the owner of Case, bought the IH farm tractor and implement divisions for a total price of $486 million.

Ironically, just a few years later, Tenneco considered selling Case because its losses were so serious. When International Harvester joined, the situation became acute, but in 1988 Tenneco decided instead to sell its oil company. After that, Case-IH as it was now known, became the largest division of the restructured Tenneco.

Chapter 7

Ford

*For most purposes, a man with a machine is better than a
man without a machine.*
Henry Ford, Dearborn, Michigan, 1926

Harry Ferguson has been described by nearly everyone, including Harry Ferguson, as brilliant. Certainly his three-point hitch was brilliant in its simplicity and effectiveness. But the usefulness of any invention is only so great as its inventor's ability to get it out into the hands of the user.

That contribution fell primarily to Henry Ford, who also considered himself a genius. According to Ford himself, his planning for a tractor preceded his planning for a car. In his 1926 book *My Life and Work*, he explained: "The automobile is designed to carry; the tractor is designed to pull. . . . The public was more interested in being carried than in being pulled; the horseless carriage made a greater appeal to the imagination. And so it was that I practically dropped work on the tractor until the automobile was in production. With the automobile on the farms, the tractor became a necessity."

For Ford, the farm tractors' future did not follow the past. Large, heavy steam tractors grew out of the theory that great weight meant great power. Yet if the tractor was to pull rather than carry, excess weight detracted from that ability to pull. Ford's tractor must be light yet strong, simple to operate yet inexpensive to buy

and maintain. Anyone who wanted a tractor should be able to get one; and having and using a tractor without difficulty was a key to Ford's— and Ferguson's—greater goal of making food and clothing more affordable as well.

Ford not only saw the handwriting on the wall, he wrote some of it himself. "The farmer must either take up power or go out of business," he prophesied. Figures from a government test with his Fordson tractor concluded that with the cost of repairs, fuel, oil, depreciation and driver's wages, the farmer spent 95¢ per acre to plow with a Fordson; feed per year of eight horses and pay for two drivers meant costs of $1.46 per acre. "Power-farming is simply taking the burden from flesh and blood and putting it on steel," Ford concluded.

Henry Ford, born in 1863, was the second generation born on farmland outside Dearborn. Grandfather John Ford emigrated from his own small farm near Cork, Ireland, in 1847, settling near relatives in Michigan and buying 80 acres. Father, William Ford, added land and expected Henry to follow the family tradition. But Henry found it all drudgery. "What a waste it is for a human being to spend hours

Palmer Fossum's 1952 Ford 8N is fitted with the Dearborn Motors Corporation Model 19–4 V-plow. Fossum's two dogs, Shena and Victor, announce visitors, escort departing guests and generally guard the Ford tractor collection.

A proud Henry Ford at the wheel of his 1907 Automobile Plow prototype. Based on a Model B car engine and gearbox, as well as components from a Model K, the Automobile Plow never made it into production. Below, the Fordson was introduced in 1916, its name a result of shortening Henry Ford & Son. It was produced in America until 1928 but Fordson remained in production in England until 1946.

and days behind a slowly moving team of horses," he said some years later. Henry preferred to tinker with machines. In 1896, his first machine ran, and in 1903, his motor company began.

Henry Ford started his first serious tractor experiments late in 1905. He established a "tractor works" just three blocks from his main plant and installed his chief engineer, Joe Galamb. Galamb was responsible for much of the design and development of the Model T gearbox. He worked through several attempts on a tractor until in 1907, a prototype using the Model B engine was sent to Ford's Fair Lane farm for testing. Two more prototypes were tested through the fall and winter. Tractor manufacture took a back seat to the automobile. His board of directors remained unimpressed and disapproved his plans to manufacture tractors at the new Highland Park plant.

In 1915, then, Ford left his own automobile company and in July 1917 incorporated his new

Ford's L-head 4x5 in. four cylinder powered the Fordson. With three speeds forward, it could cruise along at 6.8 mph in third. The 18th tractor tested by the University of Nebraska, Fordsons produced 9.34 drawbar hp. Below, the Fordson weighed 2,710 lb. yet was capable of pulling 2,180 lb. American production amounted to more than 750,000.

tractor company, Henry Ford & Son. He could not use his name alone on his tractor. Some Minnesota entrepreneurs of questionable motivation, employing a man named Ford on their staff, named their own tractor after their employee. This firm had tied up the trademark while hoping to capitalize on the confusion.

Charles Sorensen, who was for years Ford's chief palace guard and was by the late 1940s named executive vice-president of Ford Motor Company, was essentially Ford's point man on the tractor project. Ford had collected samples of virtually all his competitors' tractors. Having tested them on his farm, he moved them to the new Dearborn plant for Sorensen, Galamb, an additional engineer, Eugene Farkas, and their staff to examine. In his 1956 book *My Forty Years with Ford*, Sorensen recalled their discoveries: "All of them impressed us as too heavy and very much underpowered, so that became our first problem to solve. We also found that most of these vehicles had some outside form of drive

In the process of producing the Fordson, Henry Ford put some competitors out of business and taught the rest to trim manufacturing costs. This 1918 Fordson belongs to Dan Zilm of Claremont, Minnesota.

open to the dirt that was thrown up in farming operations. So, we decided that our tractor's drive would be inside a housing just like that on a motorcar."

Because efficient manufacture was as important to Ford as product affordability, the tractor was designed in three units: a transmission housing contained the gearbox, the differential, and the worm-wheel drive to the rear wheels; the engine included flywheel and clutch assemblies; the front end included mounts for the steering assembly and axle. Farkas planned tractor parts to support the entire machine without needing a separate frame. All these units were designed to be run on rails to a central point in the factory for final assembly.

The first production run of fifty went back to Ford's farm for testing. Sorensen and his crew corrected flaws and improved on the design. Word leaked out, and the world quickly learned that Ford's dream of ending farmers' drudgery was an approaching reality.

War had begun meanwhile in Europe. The Germans were sinking nearly a ship per day, and England was quickly losing food, able-bodied

farmers and draft animals. Lord Alfred North-cliffe, head of the permanent British War Mission to the United States, arranged to visit Fair Lane to see the tractors. Impressed, he returned to Britain to encourage production back home. He convinced Lord Percival L. D. Perry, head of British Ford Motor Company, to ask for an example.

On April 6, 1916, the United States entered World War I. The next day, Perry telegraphed Dearborn to ask to borrow Sorensen and the engineering drawings for the British government "in the national interest." Ford agreed, and within five weeks, Sorensen and five colleagues arrived with parts, patterns and implements and a goal of finding a suitable factory. By the end of June, everything was pretty much in order; then, however, order went out the window. The Germans bombed London's Fleet Street financial district, and plans changed. The proposed tractor plants were rushed into warplane manufacture, and the tractors would have to come from America.

Cables went to Ford. A deal was quickly struck, and the British government ordered a minimum of 5,000 Fordsons at cost plus $50, about $700 each. First delivery was within sixty days!

Sorensen returned home. Despite the Dearborn plant's not being ready and Highland Park's working at capacity on war material, he wasted no time. Limits in available shipping space slowed delivery, but by early December, the first Fordsons arrived in England, and according to Ford historian Allan Nevins, a total of 7,000 were shipped throughout the UK by the spring of 1917.

British agriculture was ready. *Implement and Machinery Review* magazine editorialized: "It is no longer a question of men *versus* machinery, for men are not to be had for farm work." Britain had lost 350,000 farm hands to the war effort by the time the Fordsons arrived. The food situation had grown desperate, and the government had asked that an additional 500,000 acres be cultivated in 1917.

In Ireland, where most of this land was to be plowed over, Harry Ferguson, known mostly for his exploits as an aviator and auto racer, had taken the cause of the tractor to his heart. He had begun selling the Overtime, a British derivative of the Waterloo Boy.

Harry Ferguson, the fourth child of James Ferguson, was born in 1884 and raised on the family's 100 acre farm south of Belfast. After school, Harry had his farm chores, and at age fourteen, he left school to work the farm. The steam traction engines of the time fascinated him, and anything mechanical easily lured him away from anything on the farm. Stern religious fundamentalism at home and a growing loathing for farm work set Harry to think about emigrating—escaping—to Canada. But Harry was saved when his oldest brother, Joe, hired him to apprentice at his motorcar workshop in Belfast.

Harry Ferguson found himself. He took to racing motorcycles and automobiles in the name of his brother's shop. And he won. Machines became his passion.

Ferguson succeeded in all his endeavors through his salesmanship and showmanship. By this time, he was in business for himself. As the First World War in Europe approached the United Kingdom, the necessity of food married Ferguson's enthusiasm for machines, and he entered the tractor business.

Ferguson jumped wholeheartedly into tractor demonstrations. In his biography, *Harry Ferguson: Inventor and Pioneer*, author Colin Fraser recorded the recollections of Ferguson's close friend and employee, Willie Sands: "Most of the farmers came to laugh at us. They were used to the beautiful ploughing you could do with horses and a one- or two-furrow plough, but they never bothered to think how slow and expensive it was. We only needed one furrow to run slightly shallow or slightly deep, so that the furrow slice either fell flat or stood too much on edge, and a jeer of derision went up from the farmers."

Fraser, himself an instructor on Massey-Ferguson machinery for five years, explained: "The whole matter of beautiful ploughing was in fact at the root of the British farmer's reluctance to accept tractors. The art of good ploughing was a matter of professional pride, and woe betide the ploughman whose furrows were not perfect."

The Irish government came to Ferguson. It hoped to improve tractor performance and asked him to visit farmers and perform educational demonstrations. In the next weeks, Ferguson saw mostly American imports, which he found cumbersome and difficult to use. What

Model T tractor conversions were common before and during the time of the Fordson tractor. More than a dozen companies offered kits, including the Shaw firm with its 1923 kit, above.

impressed him most, however, was the inefficiency and danger in the single-point plow hitch.

With Ireland's rocky soil, the risk of hanging up the plow on a hidden rock was great. Horses stopped moving when confronted with such a rock. Tractors with a spinning engine and flywheel tended to keep going. And often, the spinning motion simply wound around the final drive gear, bringing the tractor nose up and over on itself. It took quick reactions to depress the clutch, and Ferguson saw more than a few farmers with slower reactions missing arms or legs, or the widows of those not so fortunate as that.

Even if the impact did not flip the tractor, the plow was usually damaged afterwards.

improvement over earlier versions, which the farmers had to not only steer but also carry! These wheels also set furrow depth. Over uneven soil, with the drawbar rising and falling as the tractor moved along, the furrow height either needed constant adjustment or simply ended up sloppy and uneven.

Ferguson came to understand the tractor makers' motivation for great weight. It not only kept traction to the drive wheels but it held down the plow. But Ferguson, who had trained as an engineer at Belfast Technical College while working for his brother, was dissatisfied on behalf of the farmer.

Shaw, a California converter about which little is currently known, provided front wheels, rear wheels, a bench for seating above the gas tank, and the drawbar. The rear axle was fitted ahead of the car differential and drive was by gears. Right, other conversion kits used a chain-drive system. None was successful because the Model T had inadequate cooling capacity for use as a tractor. Fred Heidrick of Woodland, California, has painted all the parts from the conversion kit red.

Farmers were advised to use wooden sheer pins to attach the plows, but turning a field for the first time could exhaust a supply of those pins.

Another drawback resulted from using implements originally designed for horse-drawn farming. Plows had their own wheels—a vast

B ack in Dearborn, Henry Ford & Son tractor company was busy. Within three months of completing the British shipment, more than 5,000 of Ford's backlog of 13,000 American orders were already delivered. By April 1918, daily production was sixty-four. By July, 131 tractors rolled out of the Dearborn plant every day.

From his earliest tests, Ford had hoped for a tractor with a plow as a single unit. Current thinking still reflected the historical: because the plow was hitched to the horse, there was never a thought that the plow could be part of the tractor. Like unit construction, this was a new concept.

It didn't take much time to uncover some of the Fordson's shortcomings. Early Fordson design set the worm and worm gear right below the farmer's seat. Worm gears were inefficient, generating as much heat as power, and this heat transferred up the farmer's steel seat. Later versions inverted the setup and bathed the worm in oil, cooling the system and the farmer's backside. By 1920, this had largely been solved, and sales, always steady, reached 70,000 near year-end.

Meanwhile, Ford reacquired majority interest in his automobile company, and he moved Ford & Son tractors into his new River Rouge plant. Production at his Dearborn plant had reached a record 399 per day, 10,248 in September.

The war ended. The new plant had been brought up to capacity. Overcapacity caught up. Sales in the 1921 depression dropped to 36,793.

In an effort to keep production up, Ford cut the price of his tractor, then cut it again and again. He searched for the price level that would put the tractor in everyone's hands and the production level that would keep his factories busy. He began taking losses to meet those goals. The price war enraged and broke many competitors. When International Harvester brought out its Farmall and vigorously demonstrated its abilities to do tasks the Fordson could not, sales suffered enough to stop production.

So when Lord Perry stopped in on his annual visit, he saw stock piles and silenced assembly lines. He seized the moment. He proposed to Sorensen—by now head of tractor operations at Ford—that he take the machinery and dies back to the United Kingdom. Perry would use them there to build tractors where they were most needed. Ford, who wished the automobile line had shut down instead of the tractor plant, quickly agreed. It was his hope that development could continue on the unit plow.

In Belfast, Harry Ferguson and Willie Sands worked on just that. Using a Ford Model T with the Eros tractor conversion—among the better of the dozens of conversion kits available—they

Another style of Model A conversion was this 1929 machine produced by Thieman Harvester of Albert City, Iowa. Thieman, however, saved only the radiator, engine and drivetrain. These coupled to reduction gears at the rear axles. The complete tractor sold for about $500. Above, a remarkably crude affair, one of the few pieces which looked finished and professional was Thieman's decal. The extremely long wheelbase hurt maneuverability.

had their lightweight tractor. Ferguson's wheelless plow was nearly ready. Back in December 1917, he learned that a Ford tractor plant was planned in Cork, and until production was running, several thousand Fordsons were to be imported.

Ferguson was not upset by this mass-produced competition. Instead he saw it as much larger markets for his plow. And when he learned that Charles Sorensen was coming to the United Kingdom to begin the project, he grabbed drawings and raced to London.

Colin Fraser reported the scene: "Your Fordson's all right as far as it goes," Ferguson told Sorensen, "but it doesn't really solve any of the fundamental problems." Ferguson's opening remark was typical of his tact.

But Ferguson had gotten Sorensen's attention. The meeting reads differently depending on who wrote the story. Fraser related that Ferguson unrolled his drawings and explained that "achieving efficient farm mechanization lay in equipment designed on the unit principle—the implement becoming part of the tractor when it was hitched on, but being readily detachable again."

Sorensen's recollection was different: "As early as 1912, Henry Ford conceived the idea of a tractor and plow as a single unit. Like many simple things, it apparently had not been thought of before. The horse and the plow had been separate, and so, in the reasoning of the day, the tractor that supplanted the horse should be hitched to the plow. The unit tractor-plow was part of our plan when we organized to build the Fordson in 1915. In 1917, while in England, I met Ferguson, then a young machinery salesman. I told him that we proposed to combine the two. He took up the idea and in a few weeks came back with some models. . . .

"Had I been able to foresee the consequence of that meeting I would have avoided it."

The result ultimately changed tractor farming for good and for all time. But even a change this momentous was not without obstruction. Harry Ferguson Ltd. was in the business of repairing and preparing automobiles for racing and for the public roads. Harry Ferguson the man seemed perpetually in the business of improving the engineering of whatever machinery seemed most important to him at any given period of his life. Yet from the start, he shared with Henry Ford the ambition of easing the farmer's workload. Despite whatever financial motivations anyone may attribute to the two, a sense of obligation to the farmer colored the actions of both men in and out of business with each other.

Financial motivations were most prevalent among the backers of both companies. But where Ford was simply able to buy his opponents out, Ferguson was forced to make peace time and again. Ferguson's board resented the time and money spent on the development of agricultural machinery, but it appreciated the income that early sales of the Model T Eros tractor plow brought. When Ferguson and Sands attacked the development of a plow for the Fordson, the board bucked and reared like the proverbial tractor.

Ferguson persevered—exercising his greatest skill, beyond engineering and salesmanship. The result was the Duplex hitch, a design beautiful and simple in its engineering.

Attached to the tractor by two nearly parallel sets of struts, one above the other, the plow resisted the tendency to rise after impact. When firm resistance was met, the single-hitch plow tended to rise over the obstruction, or if jammed against an obstacle, the tractor tended to come up in front. This motion, from either the plow or the tractor nose, was resisted by the Duplex's upper arms, which consequently forced either the plow or the tractor nose down harder. The greater the drag, the greater the downforce.

An additional benefit was that not only could a lightweight tractor be used but also the plow itself no longer needed to be of great weight. The system's only drawback was that as the tractor pivoted over changes in the field surface, the depth of the furrow changed opposite to what the front wheels did. No draft control existed. At least not yet.

At the end of Sorensen's first meeting with Ferguson, both agreed to keep each other informed of developments. In 1920, Ferguson arranged a demonstration of his plow system. Ferguson the salesman was at his best. The Ferguson plow performed admirably. But the two principals had different goals in mind, different assessments of each other and differing views of their importance to each other. Henry Ford saw Ferguson as an innovative and effective machinery salesman, and told Sorensen to hire him on the spot. Ferguson had no desire to work for anyone else. He wanted Ford to back a plant in

Ford revolutionized the tractor with its 1939 9N. Ford's 1941 9N returned to steel wheels, the result of a rubber shortage due to wartime needs. This unique swamp paddle-wheeler is part of Palmer Fossum's collection in Northfield, Minnesota. Far right, Ferguson's three-point hitch here is attached to a Swan Rapidigger post-hole driller. Ferguson's system included integral hydraulics, which made operation of such optional tools easy. Below, the Ford 9N with Ferguson System was powered by a Ford L-head 3.18x3.75 in. four-cylinder engine. It produced 12.6 hp at the drawbar during its Nebraska tests. The 3,375 lb. tractor pulled 2,236 lb.

Eber Sherman, a New Yorker who was Ford's distributor for South America. Sherman agreed to handle sales of the plow and to help Ferguson find a manufacturer.

Ferguson's lack of success with Ford brought his backers to their feet and Ferguson to his knees. He resigned from Harry Ferguson Ltd. and opened a new shop elsewhere in Belfast.

Back in the United States, Ford's Fordson was a continuing success. Production rose to nearly 69,000 in 1922, despite a continuing postwar depression, and to nearly 102,000 in 1923. Healthy export business continued, and between 1920 and 1926, nearly 25,000 Fordsons were delivered to Russia. Ford had entered the tractor market in 1917, and by 1921, he had hold of two-thirds of the entire market. But he had not only overwhelmed his competition, he had educated it.

Barbara Marsh, in her book on International Harvester, *A Corporate Tragedy*, assessed Ford's impact: "The Fordson, much lighter than other tractors on the market, exemplified Detroit's know-how. It proved Harvester's engineers had a lot to learn about the refinements of internal combustion, heat treatment of steel, strength of materials and standardization of parts. Ford's example behooved Harvester and old-line makers of farm equipment to revamp their ancient production methods for the precision-machining requirements of the tractor."

International Harvester introduced its Farmall as a direct result of Ford's Fordson. War was declared in the farm fields, and International Harvester's engineers went right to the front lines to test and improve their product. Implements dedicated specifically to the Farmall were introduced, and International Harvester's full-line dealers sold the system. Ford had never recognized the value of his own implements.

Not only was there a profit incentive, but implements specifically meant for Fordsons would have better shown off the tractor's capabilities. Instead, farmers made do with Cockshutt or Oliver or Deere plows or other attachments. When the Fordson failed to perform as advertised or expected, the mix of manufacturers was not blamed, the tractor was. Despite falling prices, Fordson production declined, and by 1928, Ford quit selling Fordsons in the United States. IH had the lead again.

This 1941 9N was the product of Harry Ferguson's engineering and Henry Ford's production. Ferguson invented the three-point hitch that revolutionized power farming by creating the effects of a heavyweight tractor with a lightweight machine.

Ireland. Sorensen raised his offer twice, and Ford became annoyed that a modestly successful salesman would turn down such offers. Ferguson's biographer summed it up handsomely. "Both men had met their equals in stubbornness."

The plow needed some engineering cleanup. Without a depth control device, its usefulness was in doubt. Still, Ferguson made contact with

A meeting of great minds: Harry Ferguson, left, and Henry Ford examine details of the famed Ferguson System at the introduction of the Ford 9N tractor on June 29, 1939.

Ferguson continued his developments and had nearly solved the draft control dilemma. A floating skid worked in the interim until, still not satisfied, Ferguson adopted an internal onboard hydraulic lift system to ease the chore of turning the tractor at the ends of rows. By adapting a sensor to the hydraulics, by replacing more rigid mounts with ball joints and by increasing the angle of the top strut (now a single instead of a pair), he closed on the perfection he sought.

In 1925, Ferguson had incorporated in the United States with Eber and George Sherman, as Ferguson-Sherman Manufacturing, to build and market his plow. In 1928, his new three-point hitch with automatic Draft Control was ready. Yet Ford was switching over his Dearborn plant to production of his new Model A. Ferguson was caught again without a manufacturer. And then it was 1929, the stock market crashed and the Great Depression began.

Ferguson's perseverance prevailed. Reasoning that in tight money times, it might be easier to sell an idea if a manufacturer could see the idea in the flesh—or at least in steel—Ferguson ordered parts to build a prototype. Transmission pieces came from Britain's largest gear producer, David Brown. The engine, a four-cylinder Hercules, came from America. The tractor began to come together in Belfast, and when it was complete, Ferguson ordered it painted black. Some say this was because of Henry Ford's dictum that only black was suitable for cars. But Ferguson, who had little tolerance for unnecessary frills, looked on black as the most proper,

119

unadorned finish. It was only later, seeing how field dirt contrasted against the black, that he changed to gray paint.

The Black Tractor went into tests. The draft control problem still existed. Draft control was tied to the two lower links, and constant adjusting overheated the hydraulic fluid, and the system either leaked or failed. Sands was struck with an idea. Instead of using the oil under pressure on the bottom two links to position the plow and control its draft, it might work better to use the hydraulic on the top to *lift* the plow by compressing the cylinder, and let gravity take the plow down.

Success was achieved; now a manufacturer was needed. Numerous visits to David Brown solidified in Ferguson's head the idea that the gear maker should become a tractor maker. Brown finally agreed, but ultimately it was not a successful relationship there either.

The first Brown-Ferguson tractors rolled out in early 1936, and demonstrations quickly quieted farmers' skepticism. In June 1936, the first one was sold. Biographer Fraser found the buyer, John Chambers. "My father had an old Austin tractor and six horses on the farm," Chambers recalled. "But when he got his Ferguson he was able to get rid of four horses and sell the old Austin as well."

Ferguson believed his tractor could solve many of the world's problems, of hunger and overpriced garments. He set up schools throughout the United Kingdom. He craved increased production. He wanted to reduce his cost and get more of the tractors into the hands of more farmers: ease their work load, shorten their day and reduce their costs.

Allan Nevins quoted Ford in the fall of 1937: "What the world needs right now is a good tractor that will sell for around $250." In the fall of 1938, Ferguson and a small staff took a Brown-Ferguson to Fair Lane.

Ford had only reluctantly ceased tractor production ten years earlier. Fordson production continued first in Cork, then after 1933, in Dagenham, England. Yet Ford was thinking of a new, domestic Ford. Several models had been developed: one was a three-wheel row-crop type with Ford's flathead V-8; another was a four-wheel standard, in which Ford wanted an overdrive road gear.

Ferguson's timing was perfect. Ford was dissatisfied with his own engineers' work and already knew Ferguson's. The Brown-Ferguson

tractor finished its demonstration. Ford went quiet, but asked that a table and chairs be brought from the farmhouse. Ferguson had brought along a scale model to better explain his three-point hitch and draft control system,

Ford offered again to buy Ferguson's patents. Ferguson told Ford he didn't have enough money, and they weren't for sale anyway.

It remains one of the great business stories of modern history that two men, each so stubborn and each so distrusting of written contracts, consummated a deal so grand and important out of doors, in private, out of earshot of witnesses and simply on a shake of the hands.

A gentleman's agreement.

Ferguson's biography listed the conditions:

Ferguson would be responsible for all design and engineering matters and would have full authority in this respect.

Ford would manufacture the tractor and assume all risks involved.

Ferguson would distribute the tractors, which Ford would deliver to him for sale wherever and however he pleased.

Either party could terminate the arrangement at any time without obligation to the other, for any reason whatever, even if it was only 'because he didn't like the color of his hair.'

The successor to the Ford Ferguson 9N was the 2N, introduced in 1942. This 1947 version, far left, is configured as a sugar cane and cotton special. Above, the rear wheel rims are fitted with slots to allow the farmer to easily change rear-track width. Part of the sugar cane and cotton special height was achieved by using 9x40 in. rear tires. This high tricycle is part of Palmer Fossum's collection. The 120 ci engine remained unchanged from the earlier 9N specifications.

Introduced in 1948, the 8N appeared without credit to Ferguson for his three-point system, and touched off a landmark lawsuit. Above right, dozens of companies made accessories and options for the Ford N Series tractors. The grinding wheel and drill press (hidden behind the grinder) run off the PTO. Another option, the Lead-It, steers the tractor or stops it and disengages the clutch by activating the long lead arm that comes off the left front wheel. Right, the draw bar and grease gun carrier are mounted on the rear wheel fender. Just visible is the attachment for the five-bar canopy top with its adjuster. This 1950 8N touched off the desire to collect tractors: owned by Palmer Fossum now, it was once his father's tractor.

The Ford tractor plant at Dagenham would ultimately build the Ferguson System tractor on similar terms to those established for Dearborn.

All this was agreed to and sealed with a handshake. Ferguson was overjoyed. Ford was excited. Sorensen was out of town.

When Sorensen returned, he faced a done deal, the details of which Ferguson asserted with increasing frequency and vigor.

It was a short honeymoon. Sorensen's recollections were acid: "When Ferguson appeared in 1938, we were ready with a new tractor, and his plow with a hydraulic lifting device appealed to Mr. Ford. . . . We wanted him to adapt a plow to our tractor. We did not need him to show us how to build tractors—he needed us. We did want him to come with us because we knew we would make a success of his plow if we could adapt it."

Allan Nevins portrayed the decision making less caustically but still emphasized that it was Ford, not Ferguson, making design decisions. Ford invested $12 million in tooling costs and helped Ferguson finance his new distribution company.

The 9N, known as the Ford Tractor with Ferguson System, was introduced June 29, 1939. Its $585 price included rubber tires, power take-off, Ferguson hydraulics, electric starter, generator and battery; lights were optional. The 120 ci four-cylinder engine was less than half the displacement of the Fordson yet produced 28 hp at 2000 rpm. It even had an automobile-type muffler, and 9N sales brochures showed possible mounting points for a radio owing to the quietness of the engine!

Ford further improved the cantankerous Fordson by updating the ignition with a distributor and coil. An innovative system of tire mounts for the rear wheels and versatile axle mounts for the fronts enabled farmers to accommodate any width row crop work they needed, from 48 to 76 inch, using nothing more than the supplied wrench and jack. It must be presumed that this setup was a Ferguson invention, since it disappeared from the 8N tractors. But then, so did the Ferguson System badge on the Ford's radiator.

Ford had aimed for the perfect tractor with his 9N. He had tried before with the Fordson. Still, problems existed.

Palmer Fossum—a prominent Ford tractor collector today but at the time, the son of a working farmer—remembered going to a meeting at a Ford dealer in mid 1941: "They had a suggestion box and asked us to write what changes and improvements we thought they should put on a new tractor. At the end of the meeting, they opened the box and pulled out the slips. One thing we asked about were the axles. Another asked about the brake pedals, and some were having problems with the steering bearing. There was some controversy about the way the fan was blowing. Some asked about a bigger generator because they had been putting their Model A lights on the tractors and that little generator couldn't keep up."

Ford took all this to heart. By the time the 2N was introduced, Ford had fitted a grease nipple on the upper steering sector. It enlarged the cooling fan, reversed its direction and put a shroud around it.

So many Fordson owners complained of the heat on the tractor's seat that Ford made the fan on the 9N blow forward through the radiator. Fossum remembered an advertisement that said, "Now owner operator comfort thought of." Of course this didn't work because it took the engine heat and blew it back across the radiator. The 2N reversed the fan, but even that was not perfect.

The early 9N models from 1939 and 1940 came with a smooth rear axle hub. Ford poured the axle and hub in one casting, and where the two joined, sometimes an air pocket formed, causing the axle to break off from the hub under extreme situations. "Ford made a recall on those," Fossum said. "They replaced them with

Palmer Fossum has begun to collect the optional accessories made for the 8N. This tractor now sports the Cyclone air cleaner, a foot accelerator, the Sherman Bros. step-up transmission and a hand-brake lock. Below, the complicated collection of bars and levers includes the Sherman step-up transmission lever (upper left), a clutch cable (lower left) from the Lead-It (handle left center) and the PTO 'Easy Reach (center). Also visible is the five-bar canopy top and dual rear wheels and tires. Fossum has 45 of the more than 100 accessories offered.

The 8N, introduced in 1948, signified the breakup of the famous Handshake Agreement between Ferguson and Ford. With the 8N, Ferguson no longer got credit—or patent royalties—for his Ferguson system three-point hitch. Below, a symbol of the battle between Ford and Ferguson was the Dearborn Motors Corporation, Ford's tractor marketing company. Dearborn Motors also distributed accessories formerly part of the Ford/Ferguson system. Far right, with its twin stacks barking crisply to an October sunrise, the most powerful of Ford tractor accessories, a Ford flathead V-8 engine, warmed to the tasks ahead. The conversion was assembled by the industrial division of Funk Brothers Aircraft of Coffeyville, Kansas.

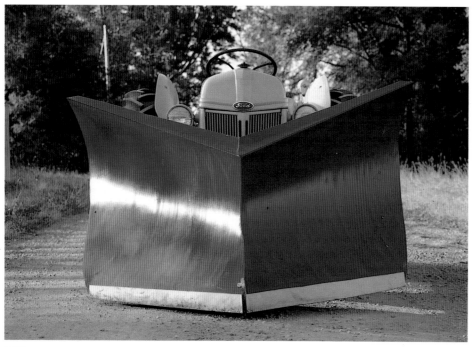

the 2N-style hot-rivetted hubs. We experienced it with my dad's 1940 tractor. In the first three years it broke off both axles. After the axle recall, many of them were destroyed, which has created a problem for the restorer now."

The brake pedals were a matter of safety. On 9N tractors, the left brake pedal and clutch were on the left side, the right brake alone was on the right. Fossum recalled the field application: "If you're turning to the left and you want to be able to ease your way around in a tight spot, you weren't able to use the brake and slip the clutch at the same time." Fossum continued and remembered the thrills: "And out on the road, if you went to stop, it would throw you because you couldn't hit the left brake *and* clutch! On 8Ns, they got both brakes together on the same [right] side."

With the introduction late in 1942 of the 2N, other changes occurred because of wartime needs for metal and rubber. Chrome instrument bezels, battery cover and radiator cap all went to steel in 1941. The easiest way for someone unfamiliar with 9N and 2N tractors to identify them is to look at the grille. The 9N and 2N had a second tag announcing the Ferguson System, but the 2N had a small 2N stamped into the Ford logo.

Ferguson again was a victim of timing, and a new world war caused orders for the 9N in 1939 and 1940 to reach barely more than half the original projection: 35,742 instead of 63,750. Production nearly touched 43,000 in 1941, but wartime rationing of rubber returned the tractor to steel wheels. The lower output raised costs, and eventually the price followed.

Nevertheless, World War II almost presented a windfall marketing opportunity for Ford. The US Government Office of Production Management (OPM) proposed cutting tractor production twenty percent while increasing repair and maintenance parts by fifty percent. Ford countered that his lightweight tractor used roughly a ton less steel than the existing large tractors. Nearly 500,000 of these older machines could be scrapped and replaced with his 9N. The savings of 500,000 tons of steel would be enough for several battleships. And Ford would make all the tractors for America.

The competition howled. Some rivals pointed out the scale of repair facility needed if one maker served the entire nation. The OPM declined Ford's offer.

Still, until the 2N arrived to replace it, the 9N made significant impact on the American farmer—just as Ford and Ferguson had hoped. More than anything, it certified the engineering ideas Ferguson had struggled to prove for decades.

Just before the Second World War, more than 6.8 million families still lived on farms. Only 1.2 million tractors, and according to a US Agriculture Department study, 17 million horses still worked the farms. Nearly one-fifth of the land under cultivation in America was devoted to feeding the draft animals, which needed to eat year-round—a fact recited regularly by Ferguson and Ford.

When Ford introduced the 8N, Ferguson's name was no longer on the tractor. Ferguson's Handshake Agreement with Ford on the lawns of Fair Lane dictated that Ford's facilities in Dagenham, England, would quickly be turned over to production of the new tractor. Yet Dagenham was virtually an autonomous entity.

Its directors had almost no obligation to change over production.

Ferguson was known throughout England as a feisty, opinionated inventor. His outspoken nature and his strong belief in his correctness put off many people, some of them in positions to do him great good. His intractability offended

Palmer Fossum's 1952 8N produced 100 hp with the Funk Aircraft V–8. Funk's ads stated, "The conversion turned a standard two-plow rated tractor into a three-plow machine, and retained all the well-known advantages of the Ford system with double the power." In fact, it was closer to three times the power.

David Brown, who built his first machines. He had rankled Sorenson. The directors of Ford Motor Co., Ltd. refused to seat him and refused to manufacture his tractor, while their Fordson continued to sell well.

The Handshake Agreement proved as good as the paper it was written on. Both sides eventually cheated on it.

When Henry Ford's son, Edsel, died in 1943, Henry, at age eighty, returned to the company to run it. His grandson, Henry II, was twenty-six and was called home from the Navy. The Ford tractor operation had already lost $20 million; the US Office of Price Administration had allowed no price increases by any manufacturer during World War I. To more closely monitor things, the tractor operation was returned to Highland Park from the River Rouge plant. Henry II directed efforts to decrease the costs.

At the same time, Henry Ford hoped to clarify his agreement with Ferguson. In 1946, Ford Motor Company tried to buy into or buy out Ferguson and to form a new sales and distribu-tion company. Tempers rose as the terms offered less and less to Ferguson: thirty percent of the new company and no royalties on the Ferguson system patents.

Henry Ford II went to his grandfather for advice. Nevins quoted the co-originator of the Handshake Agreement as saying, "Well, use your judgment. Ferguson is a hog anyway, and just keep on building the tractor."

Negotiations broke. The fourth "paragraph" of the Handshake Agreement was invoked. The agreement was dissolved. Effective December 31, 1946, Ford's agreement with Ferguson would end. Ford would continue to manufacture tractors through June 1947 for Ferguson to market, but Ford immediately established its own distribution company, the Dearborn Motor Corporation.

It was a blow to Ferguson.

Then Henry Ford died on Monday, April 7, 1947 at age eighty-three. In his lifetime, he had sent 1.7 million tractors out of his factory doors with his name on them.

Ford Motor Company, Ltd's refusal to manufacture Ferguson's tractor had led him outside by this time anyway. A 2N clone, the Ferguson TE–20, went into production in Coventry, England. The TE–20 used a Lucas electrical system. Its engine had overhead valves and a four-speed transmission, improvements that Ferguson advocated for the 9N and 2N but that Dearborn had not yet picked up.

Until the 8N. In July 1947, right after Ford's last shipments to Ferguson, the new 8N was introduced. It boasted some twenty improvements over the 2N, including a four-speed transmission. It came equipped with the Ferguson System. No royalties were paid.

"It'll be a grand fight," Ferguson said, as he filed suit against Ford. He claimed damages of $251 million.

"My God! The Marshall Plan," Ernest Breech said. Breech had been hired by Ford in 1946 to reorganize the company's finances.

Ferguson charged conspiracy to infringe on patents, to willfully destroy Ferguson's distribution business and to block manufacture of its own tractor. Ford denied or repudiated every allegation. The legal battle, not merely a patent suit but now an antitrust suit, dragged on for four years. More than 1 million pages of evidence were taken, nearly 11,000 from Ferguson himself.

Meanwhile, Ferguson had begun producing his TO–20 in Detroit. By the end of 1948, he had recorded a profit of more than $500,000, and 100 tractors per day were rolling out the doors.

So Ford countersued in July 1949, charging Ferguson with conspiracy to dominate the world tractor market, run Ford Motor Company and steal the patent ideas of his employee Willie Sands. Ford hoped to wear Ferguson down. When Ferguson's suit came to trial in March 1951, Ferguson added $90 million more to the claim to cover the Ford tractors built since filing the suit.

The trial dragged on for months until it did wear Ferguson down. On July 17, 1951, he wrote his lawyers to accept a settlement from Ford if it was offered. So, an exhausted Ferguson, who had paid lawyers $3.5 million, received $9.25 million on April 9, 1952.

Charles Sorensen later reflected on the "defeat," as he saw it: "For Ferguson, perhaps the most revealing commentary upon the justice of his cause is the fact that he was willing to accept ⅟₃₇th of his original demand."

With ground clearance to spare, even in high grass, this Model 501 Workmaster was not only built for high crops but was offset as well. Left, the 501 Workmaster engine was a 3.438x3.60 in. four cylinder with a total displacement of 134 ci. This engine was introduced in 1953 with Ford's 50th Anniversary Tractor, the Golden Jubilee.

Yet even Ferguson made use of his "victory" of the rights of the small businessperson against the giant. As Fraser surmised, "The lawsuit, with its inherent appeal to the sympathies for the underdog, must have been of inestimable value."

Ferguson's patents on much of the three-point hitch had run out by the time the suit was settled. The remaining pieces still covered had to be redesigned by Ford. But Ford was already at work developing its next tractor.

Ford's fiftieth anniversary as an auto maker was in 1953, and production of the new NAA began after the New Year. Largely restyled, the new tractor, the Golden Jubilee 1903-1953 model, quickly became known as the Jubilee.

The 8N had grown some to become the Jubilee. It was 4 in. longer and higher and about 100 lb. heavier. It also introduced Ford's new Red Tiger engine, a 134 ci overhead valve four, producing 31 hp at 2000 rpm. A new vane-type hydraulic pump replaced the Ferguson System pump, and it was relocated to the right rear of the engine. Live power take-off was optional. The Jubilee, a three-plow tractor, was produced until 1955, when Ford changed its tractor direction.

Until the introduction of the new 600 and 800 Series, five tractors in all in 1955, Ford had been a one-tractor company since 1917. Now Ford could compete more effectively against all its opponents.

LPG became a fuel option in the United States, and in the United Kingdom, diesel engines were available for the Fordson Major. Workmaster and Powermaster tractors were introduced in 1958, with model series numbers from 601 through 901. Diesel engines also came to the United States in 1958. A 172 ci four was replaced in 1961 with a 242 ci six for a five-plow-rated machine, the Model 6000.

In 1959, Ford introduced its Select-o-Speed transmission on its 881 model, using hydraulic power for gear changes in an automatic-type transmission.

In the year of Ford's Golden Jubilee, Harry Ferguson finally accomplished his childhood wish of immigrating to Canada. In 1953, he sold his tractor and plow company to Massey Harris Company in Ontario. The automobile had once again piqued his interests, and most of the proceeds of that sale, $16 million, were invested into

Ford collector Palmer Fossum of Northfield, Minnesota, far right, towers over tall grass from the operator's position on the offset 501 Workmaster. The engine was moved to the left of the tractor centerline to facilitate working with under-tractor cultivators. Its front steering wheels will turn nearly perpendicular to the direction of travel.

Palmer Fossum:
The Farmer of Fords

Two cows cry loudly. To follow the sound leads through a maze of what once housed a forty-head dairy herd.

But Palmer Fossum no longer farms dairy cows. Nor wheat nor alfalfa nor corn. Palmer Fossum farms Fords.

Where corn farmers stake out their crops with hybrid numbers identifying one seed from the next—the Garst 8952s from the Crow 498s from the Hoegemeyer 2594s—Fossum's farm does none of that. It resembles more the crop gone wild, overtaking the rural orderliness otherwise common throughout Midwest farms.

Jubilees. 9Ns. 2Ns. 8Ns. Fordsons. Fergusons. Fossum's new crop lives in the barns formerly inhabited by thirty-eight other cows. The two stragglers' cries get no response from tractors.

In the basement of the dairy barn, Ford Tractors with Ferguson Systems fill all the stalls. In back, the milking pad is now a concrete parking lot. Where cows once munched silage, Ferguson discs, Sherman plows and Dearborn harvesters and pickers now sit silently. The old tractor shed, once meant to house two or three vehicles, now is home to a dozen of the most special Fords.

Another shed to its rear, of indeterminate original purpose, now holds major portions of other significant Ford crops. These await cultivating and harvesting, fixing and reassembling.

Everywhere are Ford wheels and rims and radiators and chassis and seats and parasols and gearboxes and dash panels and front axles and differential cases and power take-off assemblies, and Ferguson hydraulics.

Another shed holds pistons and gears and camshafts and crankshafts and pinions and knuckles and halfshafts. Where Fossum formerly stored seed and fertilizers, he now guards the seeds of new restorations.

Neon signs butt up against shoulder-high pyramids of new-old-stock. For represented here is a considerable segment of the middle of Ford tractor history: the Ferguson years.

acquiring rights for the torque converter and all-wheel-drive systems. Automobile racing recaptured his attention as well, and he experimented with four-wheel drive in his own Ferguson Formula P-99, a Formula 1 Grand Prix racer.

Harry Ferguson died in his home on October 26, 1960. Less than three months before, he had contacted friends about a new idea—about getting back into the game. He wanted to build a new tractor, one that would make use of the torque converter automatic transmission and four-wheel drive.

Chapter 8

Massey

*It would be very wise if we included in the arrangement we
draw up in writing that all engineering proposals come to me
and I have control of the design of Ferguson equipment.*
Harry Ferguson, Abbotsford, England, 1953

In 1891, Daniel Massey's nearly forty-four-year-old firm, Massey Manufacturing Company of Toronto, Ontario, merged with Alanson Harris' thirty-seven-year-old company, A. Harris, Son & Company of Brantford, Ontario. Massey had begun doing repairs and fabricating rudimentary implements for the locals. Harris had done the same with his foundry, producing farm implements. When Massey-Harris Company was formed, it merged the two most successful harvesting equipment manufacturers in Canada.

A year after its merger with Alanson Harris in 1891, Massey indulged its interest in steam. It bought into the L. D. Sawyer Company, of Hamilton, Ontario, which had been producing portable steam engines since the 1860s. The infusion of Massey money expanded steam traction engine production. At the time Massey joined it, Sawyer was producing single-cylinder locomotive-type steamers. Massey-funded improvements led to the development of double-cylinder engines producing as much as 35 hp. It also brought about a name change for Sawyer, to Sawyer-Massey.

Sawyer soon advocated increasing steamer production. Sawyer-Massey had also entered the gasoline tractor market, and sketchy history suggests that a disagreement over their future direction led the Masseys to separate from the Sawyers in 1910. Curiously, the Sawyer-Massey name continued to be used into the mid-1920s. Steamers as large as 76 hp were offered, and gasoline tractors as powerful as 27–50 hp were produced. Production was ended when US imports became more attractive to Canadian farmers.

Throughout this time, Massey-Harris Company had maintained independence from Sawyer-Massey. Yet Massey-Harris had investigated gasoline engines, and in 1910, it acquired the Deyo-Macey engine company of Binghamton, New York. Engine production continued in New York until 1916 when Massey-Harris opened its own factory at Weston, Ontario.

Massey-Harris entered the tractor market much the same way that it started with stationary gas engines. In 1917, it began importing the Little Bull. The Bull Tractor Company of Minneapolis was one of the first to produce a tractor aimed at the small-acreage farmer. The designer, D. M. Hartsough, had developed the tractors that founded the Gas Traction Company, also of Minneapolis.

Prow of the Massey-Harris Model 30. Left, the Model 30 was introduced in 1947 and remained in production through 1953. Nearly 32,500 were built.

Wes Stoelk's black-and-white-face heifers inspect the intruder in their Vail, Iowa, pasture. This 1927 Wallis Model 20–30 was purchased new by Stoelk's uncle.

According to historian C. H. Wendel, Hartsough built his first tractor as an experiment in 1899. It was a single-cylinder machine, boasting 8 hp. In 1900, Hartsough built his second tractor, also a single but rated at 15 hp. While seeking financial backing, he completed his third machine with his new two-cylinder engine. His fourth tractor got him the attention he sought. Completed in 1904, it had a four-cylinder engine.

A confidential report called *The Black Book* was produced in 1915 for General Motors by Philip Rose. Rose surveyed every tractor company in business at the time. His report explained further Hartsough's development.

Hartsough's goal was to produce a machine powerful enough to pull a wheat thresher through the fields. A former North Dakota real estate developer, Pat Lyons, got the financing together, and Transit Thresher Company was born in 1907. Its first tractor, the Transit 35, used Hartsough's four-cylinder engine. Another North Dakotan, Fred Glover, bought a 35 and got himself involved in a reorganization that led to the 1908 creation of the Gas Traction Company.

The next Hartsough tractor was called the Big 4 Thirty. A remarkable plow guide was rigidly connected to the front steering wheels. Built at Gas Traction's works in Winnipeg, the Big 4 was designed as a first-time sodbuster for the northern prairies. It was marketed first by John Deere, who even approached Gas Traction to buy the firm. But Emerson-Brantingham, the Rockford, Illinois, implements manufacturer, bought the company in 1912 and picked up Glover to become tractor department manager. Emerson-Brantingham left Lyons and Hartsough to follow other directions.

Hartsough returned to the idea of a small tractor and, together with Lyons and others, began the Bull Tractor Company in January 1914.

The Little Bull was a tricycle rig that drove only one of its two rear wheels. It suffered from insufficient testing, although it had plenty of advertising pull. Some 3,800 examples were sold in its first eight months, but its lack of horsepower damaged its reputation.

So in 1915, the Big Bull was introduced. Simply an enlarged version priced at $585, it weighed 4,500 lb. and began life with a 7–20 hp rating. By 1917, its price increased to $646, and its rating increased to 12–24 hp. It retained the same configuration, but it offered variable axle height to level the tractor when plowing. This was the version that Massey-Harris imported.

Minneapolis Steel & Machinery Company contracted the manufacture for Bull. Engines were made first by Gile Engine of Ludington, Michigan, but this arrangement fell apart. So Bull founded Toro (Spanish for "bull") Motors in 1915. Yet the entire program seemed doomed. Minneapolis Steel canceled the production contract in 1917, just as Massey-Harris' importation contract began. Bull had no factory of its own, so Massey-Harris could get no tractors. One deal after another fell through. Massey-Harris had made other plans, choosing this time to manufacture for itself, under license.

Dent Parrett designed a tractor that he and his brother Henry began producing in Ottawa, Illinois, in 1913. Dent's first twenty-five sold quickly enough that he and his brother moved to Chicago and opened their doors at a former railway car repair shop. The Parretts bought engines from Buda Motor Works in Chicago and didn't chase fame and fortune. They produced one model at a time. It was their third model, the 12–25, that Massey-Harris undertook to produce in Canada. The four-cylinder Buda engine was cross-mounted, and in the United States, it sold for $1,450.

Parrett's design used automobile-type steering, and the front wheels were abnormally tall, to lessen soil compaction and increase wheel-bearing life. The larger wheels certainly put more metal down onto the dirt and rotated less frequently than did their competition. Production began at Massey-Harris' Weston plant in 1919, and the Parrett 12–25 tractor was known in Canada as the MH-1. The successor MH-2 tractor was identical except for improved rear-axle lubrication and reduced overall speed.

Massey-Harris modified Parrett's last tractor, the Model K 15–30, by repositioning the radiator against the engine. The tractor market place conspired to do in both Massey-Harris' and Parrett's efforts. Henry Ford's Fordson was being exported to Canada, and it was somewhat advanced over even Massey-Harris' MH–3. And the price wars with International Harvester in 1922 soon put Parrett out of business in the United States.

US exports to Canada became so vigorous that Massey-Harris simply withdrew for a few

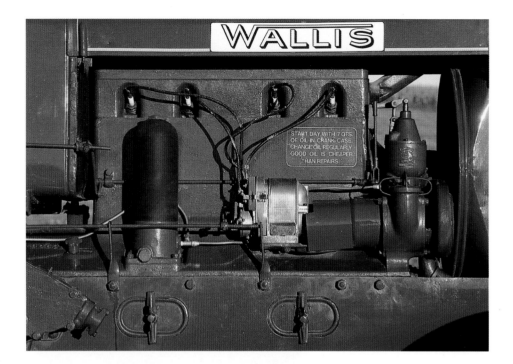

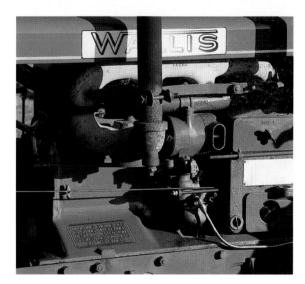

The Wallis 20–30 was tested at Nebraska and lived up to its manufacturer's reputation. It produced a maximum of 27 drawbar hp and 36 brake hp running on distillate fuel. Left, the Wallis used an American Bosch magneto. Its four-cylinder engine measured 4.375x5.75 in. bore and stroke.

years. As the post World War I economy filled out, Massey-Harris' implement lines worldwide did well. Even as the American tractor wars diminished competition by fifty percent, Massey-Harris management again felt that no tractor in its catalog meant less income on its balance sheet.

Again, Massey-Harris chose to import a US-built tractor. Despite drawbacks encountered

Wallis tractors were built by the J. I. Case Plow Works. Massey Harris purchased the company in 1928 and sold the name back to J. I. Case Threshing Machine. The most significant engineering feature was its U-frame, which enclosed and supported the engine, transmission and final drive.

chine. By 1912, Wallis saw the need for smaller tractors. Hendrickson and an assistant, Clarence Eason, sold an idea to Wallis. It earned for Hendrickson a patent for his unit-frame design, a feature that became the signature of Wallis tractors.

With the unit frame, the crankcase sump pan and transmission case were incorporated into and enclosed within a U-shaped one-piece steel casting, which also served as the frame for the tractor. This put all the moving parts inside the housing and protected everything except final drive from the dirt and elements.

Powered by a four-cylinder upright engine, it weighed 8,350 lb. It sold for $1,750 and was called the Cub.

The company was anxious to show off the Cub's reliability and dependability and organized a cross-country endurance run. The tractors left the Cleveland factory and headed west 1,000 miles to Fremont, Nebraska. When it was over, the engineering staff was impressed enough that it took over, and the tractors went on through the Midwest from county fairs to tractor exhibitions, demonstrating their strength. Wallis salespeople encouraged farmers to think of the new tractors as Thousand-Mile Cubs.

Philip Rose visited Wallis after the Cub was introduced. His criticism in his *Black Book* was prescient: "The tractor is undoubtedly one of the best made machines on the market but it is too heavy and sells at too high a price to have an extensive market."

From 1913 to 1915, Hendrickson had worked to shed more weight from the Cub. So in 1915, Wallis introduced the Cub Junior, the Model J. The J extended the boilerplate curved frame all the way to the final drive gears, fully enclosing all the running gear. Despite this additional steel but because individual housings were deleted, the J weighed about 4,000 lb. Wallis' four-cylinder engine could be specified for gasoline, kerosene or any distillate. The J was truly a junior tricycle tractor to Wallis' previous products: it weighed one-sixth as much as the Bear and sold for one-half as much as the Cub.

Most sales were already handled by J. I. Case Plow Works salespeople working out of Racine. So when the J's successor was introduced, Wallis moved to Racine as well and merged officially with Case. Hendrickson had paid attention to Ford's Fordson, and when Wallis' Model K came out in 1919, it paid homage in

with both Bull and Parrett, acquiring an existing line saved it development time and money.

Robert Hendrickson, one of Hartsough's employees at the Big 4, had designed a tractor on his own around 1908. With the help of an unidentified backer in the Pacific Northwest, Hendrickson completed his design and began testing.

Philip Rose learned of Hendrickson for his 1915 *Black Book* and gathered that about the time Hendrickson had succeeded, his financier died.

Enter H. M. Wallis, president of the J. I. Case Plow Company and a relative of Jerome Case.

Wallis Tractor Company in Cleveland, Ohio, had been an outside interest of its owner since just after the turn of the century. In 1902, the company introduced a massive tractor, the Wallis Bear. It followed conventional technology of the day, being a huge, heavy tricycle-type maone key area—it had four wheels. In the rest, it remained a J.

Three years later, in 1922, Wallis introduced the OK, an updated, improved version of the K.

Wallis advertised its tractors enthusiastically from the first days of the Cub, and bragged that it produced "America's Foremost Tractor." Certainly the celebrity of the patented unit frame, before Ford had introduced it, contributed to the legitimacy of the boast.

Wallis trumpeted the OK as "The Measuring Stick of the Tractor Industry." Its replacement sent the copywriters to the dictionary for a definition. This tractor was *certified* as to its engineering and manufacturing standards, the quality of parts used and the postproduction run-in testing to which it was subjected. An impulse starter was added. Rodger's Fuel Saving Vaporizer could now be adjusted from the operator seat. It got slightly heavier, to 4,136 lb., but in its University of Nebraska test, it pulled seventy-five percent of its weight at ninety percent of its maximum speed. Wallis' advertising certified three-plow power with two-plow weight.

Massey-Harris must have been impressed. In 1928, Wallis certified new ownership.

Negotiations had begun in 1926 to sell the OKs in Canada. A year later, these were completed, but for Massey-Harris, they led to nervous moments. At one point, Case discussed investing in Massey-Harris, and word leaked out that the Massey family was considering selling to an American firm. Vincent Massey was entering politics, and a rumor of an American buy-out could have sunk a future career.

So the Masseys quickly rounded up substantial Canadian backing and approached the negotiations from the other direction. This tactic led first to the agreement to sell Wallis (Case) tractors in Canada beginning in 1927. Efforts continued, and in 1928, Massey-Harris spent a total of $2.4 million and acquired not just Wallis but also J. I. Case Plow Works and the Case name.

Jerome Case's other business, the J. I. Case Threshing Machine Works, had no relation to the plow works except to frequently confuse farmers and investors. Massey-Harris recognized the value of a name and sold Case's name back to the Threshing Machine Works for $700,000. This move cleared up confusion, as well as some of Massey-Harris' debt, and put Massey-Harris into the forefront of full-line firms.

The next year, Massey-Harris firmed up its place in the new market, introducing the 12-20. It resembled a four-fifths scale version of the 20-30, all its external dimensions just slightly smaller. The 12-20 retained the U-frame, and both tractors sported a new shielded radiator: the 12-20 had a semicircular screen, and the 20-30 used a V-shaped screen and frame.

A new version in 1931, the MH-25, replaced the 20-30 and resulted from increasing engine speed to 1200 rpm, improving intake and combustion chamber design and changing the Rodger's Vaporizer.

The U-frame continued into the 1940s as the structural foundation of a succession of well-thought-of tractors from Massey-Harris. The MH-25 continued in production through the mid-1930s unti the Challenger and Pacemaker replaced it. The Wallis engines were improved for these, increasing power to 17-27, and a four-speed gearbox replaced the MH-25's three-speed. The Pacemaker was designed as a standard tractor, whereas the Challenger introduced a row-crop design.

Tractor styling arrived with the 1938 models. The square corners inherited from Wallis unfolded and rounded out with the Streamlined Pacemaker. Wallis' green paint scheme disappeared too with the introduction of Massey-Harris red. Rubber tires were optional.

For 1940, Massey-Harris replaced both the standard Pacemaker and row crop Challenger with Twin-Power versions. This feature overrode the 1200 rpm governor on drawbar work to provide 1400 rpm engine speed for the drive belt. Orchard tractors, introduced with the 20-30, were once again available in Twin-Power tractors. An optional power implement lift was offered.

The Twin-Power tractors established Massey-Harris as a certified success. The Wallis legacy provided reliability owing to the sealed running gear, and the tractors' consistent performance in the Nebraska tests built a faithful following.

Perhaps because of the success of the company's Wallis line of tractors, Massey-Harris' engineers took a risk. Borrowing virtually nothing from Wallis, Massey-Harris introduced its General Purpose (GP) model in 1931.

The GP broke new ground in small tractors because it applied power to all four wheels. It was an attempt to lure farmers away from

The most significant engineering feature of the Wallis tractors was the U-frame. This heavy steel plate enclosed and supported the engine, transmission and final drive. It sealed moving parts from dust and supported the mass without an additional frame.

crawlers or to appeal to farmers who had considered much larger tractors to solve their pulling problems. Massey-Harris' innovative alternative used equal-size wheels all around.

Before this time, four-wheel-drive attempts had been unsuccessful. The complexities of dual differentials and steerable drive axles produced a tractor that was difficult to maneuver, a problem that virtually defeated the virtues for which four-wheel drive was sought.

Massey-Harris fitted the Hercules 15–22 hp four-cylinder to the GP. For its weight, it didn't produce as much power as some of Massey-Harris' own two-wheel-drive machines.

Options included electric lights and starter, power take-off and even an orchard configuration. The GP was basically a row-crop tractor, and tread width was available from 48 to 76 inches, with nearly 30 inches of ground clearance.

As Michael Williams pointed out in his *Massey-Ferguson Tractors*, the unorthodoxy may have contributed to the GP's failure. In the 1930s, horses were still a major motive force in row-crop farming. Their replacement was a sore subject among farmers wary of costs and leery of

machines. Massey-Harris' brochure explained that the GP "was designed to actually replace horses in the corn and cotton belt under any soil conditions."

Furthermore, a four-wheel drive was perfectly suited to steeply hilly terrain, but it was not yet common to plant row crops on challenging hillsides.

In 1936, the GP was offered in gasoline or kerosene versions. Even wider tread width was available, and rubber tires were offered. In an attempt to address the insufficient power problem, Massey-Harris offered the six-cylinder Hercules engine, though it is not exactly certain whether this was done at the factory or at the local dealer. Fewer than a dozen of these were produced, and even this option didn't increase interest in the little four-wheel drive.

By 1937, the GP was out of production. With it Massey-Harris had jumped about twenty-five years ahead of the time. The tractor simply needed continued development.

With the end of the 1930s, Massey-Harris continued its prescience. Just as Henry Ford was introducing his 9N, Massey-Harris brought out its 101 Junior. A small two-plow-rated tractor, it was priced at $895, which included a self-starter and battery ignition, rubber tires and fenders. The company's Twin-Power feature was optional.

Unlike Ford's 9N, the 101 constituted a full line, with Standard, Super and Senior versions as well as the Junior. Massey-Harris numbered these models by their engines: 101, 102, 201, 202 and 203 tractors. Yet it continued to use outside sources for power.

The Junior and Standard used a Continental four. More interesting were the MH Senior, the Super and the 201, which used a six-cylinder Chrysler truck engine modified for Massey-Harris. Six-cylinders were a legacy from the Hercules attempt with the GP-4WD, and they were quite a luxury in the days when John Deere still stood by its two-cylinder Poppin' Johnnys, and everyone else got along on four.

Massey-Harris believed in the advantages. It boasted in its advertising that Chrysler's truck engines had more than 12 billion miles of proven performance, and with Chrysler engines, Massey-Harris offered the widest-ranging dealer service network of any tractor manufacturer.

The small tractors, the MH-101, the Junior and the Standard, were supplemented by a wartime military version, the MH-81, and by the General. The MH-81 apparently turned few furrows but was used extensively by the Royal Canadian Air Force to turn aircraft. The General was another Massey-Harris product built under license, but this was an odd arrangement.

The General was a product of the Cleveland Tractor Company, parents of the Cletrac crawler. It was Cleveland Tractor's only effort into the wheeled market. A tricycle high-clearance row-crop configuration, it used a Hercules four-cylinder rated at 10-17 hp. Massey-Harris' other tractor efforts and its great success with its implements at the time may well have diffused its interest in the General; even though Massey-Harris dealers sold it, it was never painted red—remaining Cletrac Yellow—and it never bore Massey-Harris' nameplate. It remained in catalogs only two years.

In 1946, a new full range of tractors was introduced. Massey-Harris engines powered the 55 and 44, the top of the new line-up. Between the 44s built in Racine and its British kin, the 744, the tractor was a great success. Production peaked at nearly 25,000 in 1951, and the 44s

The Wallis 20–30 weighed 4,523 lb. This classified it as a lightweight tractor during the period.

constituted half of Massey-Harris' tractor sales in 1950 and 1951.

Massey-Harris' factory in Marquette, France, produced a small machine, the Pony. An attempt to enter the one-plow market, it did well in France and Europe, although the existing competition from Allis' G and the Deere's L from the United States overwhelmed it at home in Canada.

"Technology catch-up" is a key element of the tractor business through North American history. Few innovations caused more competitive catch-up than Harry Ferguson's System, incorporated in the Ford N Series tractors. His automatic Draft Control and increased plow downforce was a tremendous sales advantage to Ford. All the other manufacturers worked feverishly to duplicate its effect without violating its patent.

Massey-Harris' system was called the Depth-O-Matic hydraulic lift, and it was first

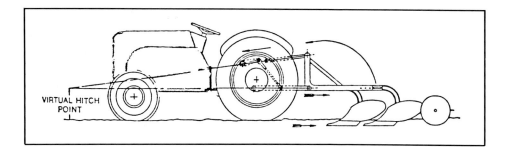

VIRTUAL HITCH POINT

The mechanical forces at work on Harry Ferguson's automatic draft control. The system was first incorporated into the Ford 9N tractor, and was later copied at least in some form by every tractor maker that wanted to stay in business.

offered as an option on the MH-20 and 30 around 1950. Massey-Harris' hydraulics were not an internal, integral system but an add-on, and the Depth-O-Matic didn't have Ferguson's automatic Draft Control.

The distance between Massey-Harris' system and Ferguson's led Massey-Harris to hire Arnold Pitt, a physics professor at the University of Toronto, to head a research department within engineering. Pitt was asked to develop a Ferguson System for Massey-Harris, to attach and control the implements as well as Ferguson's.

Pitt failed. Massey-Harris' president, James S. Duncan, began thinking of the necessity of an agreement with Ferguson. By the middle of 1953, Duncan recognized that neither its Depth-O-Matic nor Pitt's tractor attempt came close.

Harry Ferguson had worked with Henry Ford for several years, introducing in 1939 the Ford Tractor with Ferguson System. Two strong-willed men had gone into business on a handshake done in the middle of a farm field, and before ten years had passed, the agreement was as completely overturned as any soil to come beneath a Ford-Ferguson tractor.

As the Ford-Ferguson partnership unraveled, Ferguson introduced his own tractor, first in England and then in the United States. When Ford introduced the final tractor in the series begun with Ferguson, it incorporated Ferguson features without paying any royalties. Ferguson sought fair recompense, and in the end, the sum of $341 million seemed fair enough. Ford fought back in federal court, and a settlement left Ferguson with a tiny percentage, 9.25 million.

By then, however, Ferguson's own tractors, known as TE-20s, were outselling Fords in Great Britain, and in the United States, the TO-20 met ready acceptance among farmers who knew the name from Ford's 9N and 2N tractors.

All through his tractor business career, Ferguson had followed a consistent plan. He arranged with manufacturers to produce his gray tractors from his designs while he took care of their distribution and sales. He had always preferred doing the demonstrations for farmers to dealing with the daily hassles of manufacturing. When his agreements with Ford began to fall apart, Ferguson—even as he organized his patent infringement suit against Ford—began looking around for another North American producer. At one tractor demonstration to potential backers in 1947, he met Jim Duncan, president of Massey-Harris.

Duncan had grown up with Massey-Harris implements. His father was Massey-Harris' first import agent in France. Duncan had joined Massey-Harris himself when he was seventeen and proceeded to work for the company in Germany and Argentina as well as France and Canada. In 1935, Duncan became general manager. By 1944, he was president.

While Ferguson extricated himself from Ford, Ferguson's engineers in England kept at work on other projects that interested Massey-Harris in Canada. Colin Fraser, author of *Harry Ferguson: Inventor and Pioneer*, uncovered the birth of their merger.

By June 1953, Ferguson sought to manufacture a tractor-mounted removable harvester. The power system of the harvester—meaning the tractor—could be used for planting, cultivating and other purposes during the rest of the year. Massey-Harris people met Ferguson people to discuss Massey-Harris' producing it.

At the last minute, Ferguson vetoed the plans but asked Duncan to visit him at his home. Duncan knew about Ferguson and heard the inventor out. Ferguson startled Duncan by first trying to hire him and then by offering to sell Duncan his own business. Duncan knew the merger being offered was unlike any other in Massey-Harris' history. Every competitor had tried to better Ferguson's System; they all failed, and the best they could manage was to steal it, copy it or license it. Massey-Harris had the opportunity to get not only the system but the creative mind behind it.

Ferguson had his own ideas, and they included a new gray tractor, basically an enlarged TE-20 nicknamed the Big Fergie, something hinted at in the Ford years but never followed through. Ferguson offered to sell Massey-Harris the entire company; Duncan had prepared. He recited Massey-Harris' offer, and Ferguson agreed.

Sometime later that day, Ferguson created the first of his loopholes in the deal. Ferguson asked for an honorary role in the new company, so Duncan agreed to name him chairman of the company.

Days later, Ferguson approached Duncan with the acknowledgment that Duncan, as financier, had little understanding of engineering matters. So why didn't Ferguson just handle approval of all engineering matters and projects? In that way, Duncan would always have an escape when asked for a decision. Massey-Harris' board agreed to that too.

One final loophole was a misunderstanding of purchase price when converted to English pounds from Canadian dollars. The discrepancy came to $1 million, and after much squabbling and bargaining, Ferguson offered an old Irish solution to any problem, the toss of a coin. The negotiators blanched but agreed, knowing the Ferguson name alone might be worth it. Ferguson tossed, called tails and lost.

Ferguson sold his company for 1.8 million shares of Massey-Harris stock, worth nearly $16 million. He was the largest single stockholder in the resulting company, Massey-Harris-Ferguson. Gray tractors joined the reds.

Duncan's two loopholes returned quickly to haunt him. Conceived in England, Ferguson's Big Fergie, the TE–60, left out sizable markets in the United States because no tricycle version was planned. Duncan specified some changes, including using outside engines to reduce costs.

At the same time, Ferguson's Detroit plant designer Hermann Klemm had completed a TE–20 replacement, the FE–35, specifically for production in America. Ferguson got riled, suspecting Massey-Harris' North American management of supporting Ferguson's North American team in an inferior machine. In an attempt to make peace, Duncan agreed to manufacture a tractor based on the TE–60 for marketing by Massey-Harris dealers.

Ferguson felt another slap in the face; Massey-Harris tractors were so far inferior to his that he thought *they* should be dropped from the Massey-Harris-Ferguson line. Smarting, he resigned.

Duncan, tired of challenges to every decision, accepted. Massey-Harris bought back Ferguson's stock, requiring in exchange that Ferguson remain out of the tractor business for the

Clarke Hall of Elmwood, Nebraska, bought his 1931 Massey-Harris General Purpose four-wheel-drive in the late 1970s as a working tractor. But the rarity of its engine caused him to start showing it. It is one of the 12 known to have been built with the Hercules engines. Left, the 4.00x4.50 six-cylinder engine transformed the GP from a two-plow-rated tractor into a three. Standard power was a Hercules four and so much horsepower was lost through gears and differentials that the advantage of four-wheel-drive was also lost. Only two GPs with Hercules sixes are known to exist.

next five years. Ferguson, age seventy, agreed. His interests were already directed to four-wheel drive and to automobiles. He acquired the rights to the invention of Italian Count Teramala, for a torque converter. He paid about $1.4 million and began working on its application in automobiles.

Perhaps to placate loyal customers, Massey-Harris-Ferguson continued to operate for some

In its Nebraska test, the Massey-Harris Model 30 with its Continental 3.440x4.375 in. four cylinder produced 20.6 drawbar hp and 33 belt hp. The 3,667 lb. tractor pulled a maximum of 3,273 lb. This 1947 Model 30 row crop is part of the collection on display at the Antique Gas and Steam Engine Museum at Vista, California.

time as two separate competing companies, Ferguson versus Massey-Harris. Ferguson's Detroit factory had been producing the TO-30 tractor since 1951. Its replacement, somewhat overdue, arrived in early 1955, as the TO-35 and the TE-35 for Europe. A new gearbox gave six speeds, and live PTO was optional. The TO-35 was delivered in Ferguson Gray, bearing the Ferguson name, to the former Ferguson distributors. A red version was introduced at the same time, called the MH-50. It carried familiar MH lines outside, but below the sheet metal it was much like the Ferguson.

Nearly a year later, the MH-50 introduced Hydramic Power—basically the Ferguson System with a different name. Also in 1956, the MH-33, 44 and 55 models were updated as MH-333, 444 and 555 models, now with Depth-O-Matic hydraulics (the Ferguson System), power steering and a two-speed transfer case.

Another fraternal twin was born for Ferguson dealers; the F-40 was their version of Massey-Harris' tricycle row-crop MH-50.

Then in 1957, the MH-50 was replaced with the MF-50; the gray TF-35—English market TO-35—was repainted red and called the MF-35; and a new tractor with a Perkins diesel,

the MF-65, was introduced worldwide. The MF-65 rated 50.5 hp and offered disc brakes and live PTO.

Alanson Harris' name was withdrawn from the logo in 1958, completing the amalgamation. The company was now Massey-Ferguson.

The same year, the legacy of Wallis' Thousand-Mile Cubs was resurrected. Sir Edmund Hillary took three track-fitted TE-20s 1,200 miles to the South Pole. And in warmer climates, Massey-Ferguson's factory in France introduced a new small tractor, the MF-25, and the North American market got its first MF-85s. The 1958 line ranged from 25 hp to 60 hp in gas or diesel versions.

But customer demand edged toward larger, more powerful machines. Massey-Ferguson once again sought outside sources, and Minneapolis-Moline built a 425 ci six-cylinder for the MF-95.

In 1959, Massey-Ferguson acquired F. Perkins Ltd. of Peterborough, Ontario. Frank Perkins had established his diesel engine company in 1932, employing Charles Chapman as chief engineer. The two had worked together at Aveling & Porter, in Aveling, Kent, England. Chapman designed the Invicta diesel, which set a 977 hour plowing record before being accidentally shut off (when it was quickly restarted, it ran another 600 hours continuously). When Aveling & Porter went bankrupt, Perkins opened his own shop. He began supplying Massey-Harris in 1947 with his P6 engine going into the MH–44 and 744 tractors.

Massey-Ferguson acquired an Italian tractor company, Landini, in 1960. It had used diesel engines from its start in 1910.

Giovanni Landini began as a blacksmith in 1884 in Fabbrico, Italy. His implements led to a single-cylinder stationary engine in 1910. In 1924, when Landini died, his sons took over and introduced tractors. Their first successful tractor ran in 1925, as a single-cylinder semidiesel. These extremely inefficient engines required enormous displacement to produce little power. Landini's 1932 tractor rated at 40 hp was a single-cylinder of nearly 858 ci. Their advantage was that they ran on almost anything flammable. When the replacements came in 1955, they too used Perkins diesels. In 1957, Landini introduced its C 25 crawler, which Massey-Ferguson picked up when it acquired the company.

In November of 1959, former Ferguson employee Albert Thornbrough was invited to visit Harry Ferguson. Thornbrough had become the president of Massey-Ferguson. He saw a new tractor at work. Ferguson had successfully incorporated a limited-slip differential onto a tractor. Thornbrough was intrigued and recommended the Massey-Ferguson's board look into it.

But then, on October 25, 1960, Harry Ferguson was found dead in his morning bath. He was seventy-six.

For decades, Ferguson had blended genius engineering with the insecurity and impatience of the genius artist inside him, but not always successfully. Seldom at peace within, he suffered fits of depression as his inventions rose and fell in acceptance and recognition. He knew he was right nearly all the time and admitted that his associates could be right some of the time.

Ferguson spent his life pursuing "that which performs perfectly the function for which it was designed and has no superfluous parts." Perhaps this is the explanation of his lifelong difficulty in business.

His tractors, indeed nearly all his inventions, met his expectations. His associates could not.

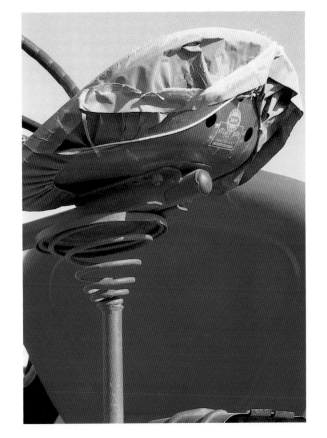

Tractor seats were notoriously uncomfortable, especially after the first day's work. Massey-Harris padded its seats and, like many competitors, developed a spring suspension. Below, five forward speeds were offered, with top gear providing more than 12.5 mph. A feature called Twin-Power bypassed the governor at 1,500 rpm and allowed the engine to run 1,800 rpm on the belt or in top gear.

Chapter 9

White

*You may remember there was a peculiar "animal?" in the
[Popeye] cartoons which was part fowl and part animal,
supposed to live on orchids. No one knew what to call it but it
knew all the answers and was referred to as a Jeep.*
W. C. MacFarlane, president of Minneapolis-Moline,
explanation of the origination of the name Jeep,
1942

In February 1962, when White Motor Corporation acquired Cockshutt Farm Equipment, White had only been in the farm equipment business for fifteen months. It had owned the Oliver Corporation only that long.

Within another twelve months, it folded into itself the Minneapolis-Moline Power Implement Company. And six years later, to reorganize corporate pressures, the White Farm Equipment Company was spun off. It landed in Oakbrook, Illinois, an exclusive corporate headquarters community 30 miles west of Chicago and 30 miles east of the nearest tillable soil.

To any student of farm history, financial reorganization and merger are events as familiar as harvesting. If these were charted carefully with White, they probably happened almost as often as harvesting. In all, the corporate conglomerate make-up of White Farm Equipment was a stunning forty-eight companies during a period of 160 years.

Frost & Wood Company, founded in 1839, produced tillage and harvest implements for ninety-four years. James G. Cockshutt's company, Cockshutt Farm Equipment, founded in 1877, thirty-eight years after Frost & Wood, waited another fifty-six years before taking Frost & Wood over. Both were a part of this story.

Abell Engine & Machinery Works and Acme Steel were a part of it, as were Universal Tractor and US Steel. Henney Buggy, Freeport Carriage and Mandt Wagon all joined Moline Implement just after the turn of the twentieth century.

Herzog Manufacturing gave birth to Gillette-Herzog in 1882; which gave birth to American Bridge Company in 1890; which sunk into US Steel in 1902, but not until yielding twins— Minneapolis Malleable Iron, which married Twin City Iron Works, and another offspring, still named US Steel, which left the farm business to follow interests in the big cities.

The year was now 1903. Superior Drill— born of the parents of Thomas, Ludlow & Rodgers in 1860, seeders of the broadcast and drill variety—set up housekeeping with Hoosier

By the time White Farm Equipment was formed in 1969, it incorporated generations of corporate mergers and buyouts; the trademark of the Minneapolis Threshing Machine Co. was just one of the firms to go into the group. Left, Minneapolis-Moline's most distinctive tractor, the U-DLX Comfortractor.

Drill, and Bickford & Company got together with Brennan & Company. They all moved in with A. C. Evans, P. O. Mast and the Empire Drill Company, joining American Seeding Machinery Company.

Then in 1929—a year that was good for farm implement mergers but not so good for the economy in general—American Seeding Machinery joined Nichols & Shepard Company, Hart-Parr Tractor Works, McKenzie Manufacturing and the Oliver Chilled Plow Company (né South Bend Iron Works, born 1868) to form a new, improved Oliver Farm Equipment Company.

Minneapolis Steel joined Minneapolis Threshing Machine Company and Moline Implement, born of Champion Reaper in 1918, and this ménage à trois begat Minneapolis-Moline Power Implement Company, born in 1929, in Minneapolis.

Each of these great-grandchildren of the farm implement evolution reorganized and expanded and contracted between 1929 and the early 1960s. Oliver Farm became Oliver Corporation, Cockshutt became Cockshutt Farm Equipment Company of Canada and Minneapolis-Moline Power Implement Company swapped away power implements for incorporation. Between 1944 and 1960, Oliver bought and sold Cleveland Tractor, and in 1951, Minneapolis-Moline bought B. F. Avery.

The desire of every one of these acquisitions and mergers, separations and divestitures was to be more competitive and to broaden the product line so that the farmer didn't have to leave the family to fill any farm machinery needs.

Cleveland Tractor Company began life as the Cleveland Motor Plow Company back in 1917 when Rollin White, of the White Motor Company, founded it. White had made his name with sewing machines. His machinery interest led him to produce steam-powered automobiles at the turn of the century. As his engineering and financial interests broadened, he used his new company to experiment with crawler tractors.

Cleveland Motor Plow's first crawler, the Model R, was advertised as the tractor "geared to the ground." The R used an outside-sourced Wiedley four-cylinder engine and rated 10 hp. Within a couple years, Cleveland Tractor was producing its own engines. The tracks were driven through differentials and planetary gears. To steer the tractor, track brakes were pulled against the main gears to slow one side while the other pulled.

White renamed the company the Cleveland Tractor Company, and by 1918, Cletrac was born. That year's Model H rated 12-20 hp and enclosed the lower track rollers in metal sheathing. In the early 1920s, Cletrac continued with smaller machines, the Model Fs with humpback-style tracks, rating 9-16 hp. By the late 1920s, Cletrac had gone outside for engines, as its tractors grew in competition with everyone else. The 12-20, the Models 30, 40 and 100 all used Wisconsin four- and six-cylinder engines. The numbers represented the drawbar horsepower.

Cletrac added diesels in 1933 with its Model 80 and in 1934 with its Model 35, using Hercules six-cylinder engines. The company introduced its Model E, in track widths from 31 to 76 inches in 1935. In 1939 and 1940, Cletrac produced its nontracked tractor, the GG, a row-crop tricycle with 14-20 hp from the Hercules four-cylinder; this machine was picked up by Avery, after 1942.

In 1944, Oliver purchased Cletrac; Oliver crawlers were still produced in the old Cletrac factory opened by White in 1917. Ironically, White purchased Oliver in 1960, reacquiring Cletrac, which was then moved to the former Hart-Parr works in Charles City, Iowa, until the crawler line was finally dropped in 1963.

I gnatius Cockshutt, an Englishman from York, arrived in Brantford, Ontario, as an advance scout for his father, who had opened a general store in Toronto and wanted to expand. In 1829, Brantford, about 60 miles southwest of Toronto, was a small community of just 200. Ignatius settled and prospered, married and raised a family. In 1877, when Brantford became a city, Ignatius became a business partner with his son, James, cofounding the Cockshutt Plow Company, located on Market Street and employing five.

Hart-Parr's single-overhead-camshaft 10x15 in. twin used a single cam lobe to operate both the intake and exhaust valves. The hit-and-miss ignition system tended to fire both cylinders in quick succession, followed by several sparkless compressions.

Established as a plow manufacturer, the Cockshutts added other lines to their implements, and their business flourished. In 1893, Cockshutt was incorporated. In 1911, it had grown to the extent that it went public with a stock offering.

By 1924, Cockshutt had tractors in its catalog, marketing Hart-Parr tractors in Canada. In 1928, a year before Oliver acquired Hart-Parr, Cockshutt came to an agreement with Allis-Chalmers to market its tractors in Canada, and a 1931 sales brochure listed Allis-Chalmers Model 20-35 and its United tractors with Cockshutt nameplates. Cockshutt also represented Frost & Wood Company and merged with it in selling its implements in 1933.

Following several years of agreement with Allis-Chalmers, through roughly 1933, the arrangement soured. By 1934, Cockshutt was back in business importing tractors, marketing Olivers in Canada through the late 1940s.

The 1913 Hart-Parr "Old Reliable" flywheel weighed 1,140 lb. With an engine speed of 300 rpm, the power generated by the flywheel alone is considerable. Gary Spitznogle of Wapello, Iowa, restored and owns this 1913 Model 30–60. The steering system is variously described as a "tight-and-loose-chain" or a "bolster-and-chain" system. Either way, it meant plenty of anticipation was necessary to make a turn.

According to Robin Kirby, a Cockshutt historian and former employee, the first tractor entirely Cockshutt's own was the 1947 Model 30. In 1944, Cockshutt engineers had bought as many as a dozen examples of tractors built by other makers to tear apart and examine. They looked at good and bad features to adopt the best to ideas of their own. Discussions took place with several outside engine manufacturers and models were tested with Buda, Continental, Waukesha and Perkins engines. Cockshutt even investigated the possibility of manufacturing a tractor jointly with Massey-Harris, but this was ruled out as too costly. Eventually Buda was chosen, and an architectural designer, Charlie Brooks, created the slender, almost delicate Model 30, which put Cockshutt on the tractor makers' map.

Several years of intense testing yielded a reliable machine and introduced a landmark improvement in tractor power sources, the continuous live power take-off. Before Cockshutt's innovation, when the tractor was slowed or stopped or the clutch disengaged, the PTO would slow or halt. Cockshutt rendered the PTO independent, with its own separate clutch. In this way, harvesting machinery or other PTO-dependent implements would continue to operate even if the tractor was stationary.

The Model 30 was offered with gas, diesel or LPG Buda engines from the start. In 1949, Cockshutt brought out the Model 40 with a Buda six-cylinder, also in gas or diesel. Continental's 20 hp engines powered the 1951 Model 20s, and in 1953, the Model 50 was introduced. Kirby said the Model 50 used the Buda 40 hp engine with the cylinder liners removed. All other specifications remaining the same, the larger bore added nearly 10 hp.

When Allis-Chalmers purchased Buda engines, its agreement with Cockshutt was ended and the proliferation of engines read like a who's who. Continental engines powered the 20s and rated nearly 30 hp, so the Model 30 was dropped and replaced with the Model 35 with a Hercules engine. Perkins engines fired the Model 40, with the diesel leading to a new Model 40D4, for Perkins' four-cylinder diesel powerplant.

For decades Cockshutt had been a successful farm implement manufacturer. Its catalog showed a full line of seeding-to-harvesting machinery. It marketed its products in the United States through the National Farm Machinery Cooperatives, based in Bellevue, Ohio. In 1951, Cockshutt purchased the Cooperative. Among other equipment marketed under license for National Coops were the Golden Eagle and Black Hawk lines of tillage and harvest equipment. Cockshutt then introduced for its US markets its Golden Eagle and Black Hawk 20, 30 and 50 tractors.

The year 1951 saw other subtle changes in the tractors: the year of manufacture was deleted from the tractor serial number—at the request of dealers presumably getting caught selling last year's tractors—and the Deluxe series was introduced, with brighter two tone paint schemes, a padded seat and an optional cigarette lighter! As reported by Kirby, the assembly line personnel hated the Deluxes because of the extra work in changing colors.

Outside industrial design came to Cockshutt. In 1957, the company introduced the 500 Series, designed by Raymond Loewy's group. The art deco stylishness of the first-series Cockshutt tractors was traded for more purposeful lines, as the bodies widened, the grilles became bolder and more masculine, and the entire machine took on a heavier, more massive appearance. Problems with production delayed the introduction, but within a year, the 540 gas, the 550 gas or diesel, and the 560 Super and 570

Super gas or diesel were in production and deliveries began. An engineering project, the 580 Super, engendered only three prototypes before the experiment was shelved.

In 1962, Cockshutt was purchased by White Motors for its subsidiary, the Oliver Corporation, and although production continued for more than a decade with implements and tractors under the Cockshutt label, the company's identity was absorbed into Oliver.

The University of Wisconsin at Madison gave birth to another White grandparent. Two students in engineering designed their first engine while still enrolled. After graduation they had no financial backing to put their three-year-old engine designs to practical use. Charles W. Hart and Charles H. Parr left Madison for Charles City, Iowa. The year was 1900.

Whether it was superstition or not, the move to the city of their name was successful. By 1902, their first gasoline traction engine, a 17–30

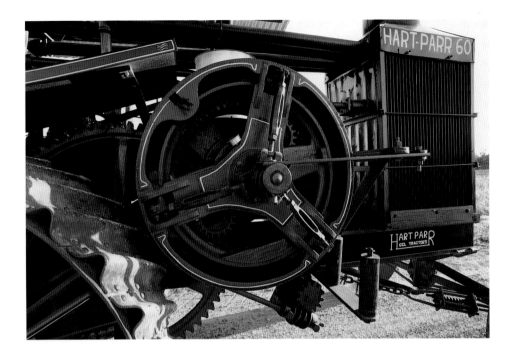

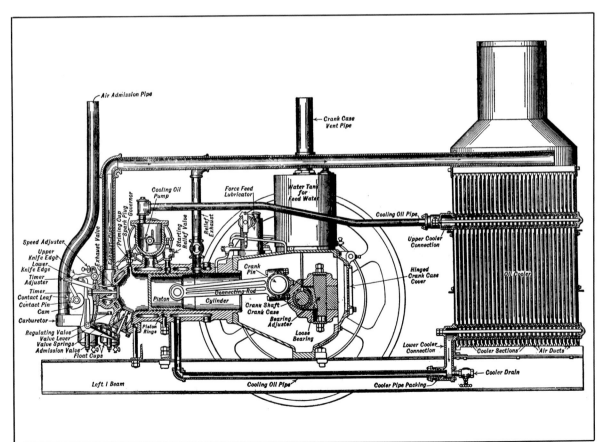

"Old Reliable" rated 60 hp on the drive belt pulley, but with the engine mass it had behind it, the torque must have been considerably greater. Its one-speed transmission gave it a top speed of only 2.3 mph. Left, a sectional drawing of the Hart-Parr 30–60 "Old Reliable," in production from 1907 through 1918. The horizontal twin 10x15 in. engine produced 30 drawbar hp at 300 rpm. Oil cooled, it was started on gasoline and then switched over to kerosene.

147

The Hart-Parr 30–60 was powered by a horizontal two-cylinder 10x15 in. single-overhead-camshaft engine. The engine was designed to burn any fuel including alcohol.

hp rated machine, was tested in the fields and improved in their city shops. Their second model, a 22–45 hp version, introduced in 1903, was successful enough from an engineering point of view that a production run of fifteen was completed. Banker M. W. Ellis backed Hart and Parr, and became a substantial stockholder and their financial adviser.

Hart-Parr continued development and introduced an 18–30 in 1903. A 17–30 hp production version was offered from 1903 through 1906. Then in 1907, Hart-Parr introduced its 30–60, Old Reliable, and its advertising manager, W. H. Williams, introduced the first commercial use of the word tractor in promoting Old Reliable.

Hart-Parr's machinery was derivative of the styles of steam traction engines of the day. It was heavy. Flywheels weighing 1,000 lb. and tractors

weighing 20,000 lb. were Hart-Parr trademarks. Two-cylinder kerosene engines were cooled by oil, and make-or-break ignition systems popped only on demand as the engine load increased or decreased. The tractors were driven and steered by chains and moved at a stately 2.3 mph. Steering required plenty of forethought.

Horsepower increased and tractor size followed. A 40–80 hp tractor was offered from 1908 to 1914, with an improved ignition system. A monstrous railway-locomotive-sized 60–100 hp prairie sodbuster reportedly weighed more than 50,000 lb. and was in Hart-Parr's catalog only in 1911 and 1912.

By this time, Hart-Parr had another innovation. Its early years of failure at the hands of uneducated operators led it to start instruction programs. Instruction by mail was available for those who lived nowhere near the branches. An idea whose time had arrived, this was adopted rapidly by competitors who had suffered similar expensive repairs owing to operator ignorance or carelessness.

Hart-Parr, leading some trends, followed others, and introduced its first small tractor in 1914. The 15-22 hp Little Red Devil was a peculiar tricycle rig. It was propelled by its large single rear wheel, with a direct-drive reversible two-cycle two-cylinder engine. At slowest idle, the timing lever was reversed and the engine would misfire itself into running backwards. Historian C. H. Wendel suggested that this odd configuration demonstrated how much more practical and reliable Hart-Parr's other larger, heavier tractors were to own and operate. Still, at its peak production Hart-Parr turned out five Little Devils a day, and at $850 each, more than 1,000 sold. The model was dropped in 1916.

Hart-Parr did recognize the trend and in 1918 introduced two much more practical smaller tractors, the 15-30 Type A and the New Hart-Parr 12-25. Both still ran with two-cylinder engines; however, in 1921, the 10-20 Model B two-cylinder was offered as a 20-40 model, which Wendel characterized as being essentially two Model B engines side by side.

Sometime in 1919, Hart and Parr sold out to their partner Ellis but remained in Charles City and continued working. The engineering improved steadily from the mid-1920s. Disk clutches appeared, forced-lubrication systems were adopted, the Robert Bosch high-energy magneto was fitted, water injection was added to the kerosene engines to eliminate preignition and three-speed transmissions were used.

Within a few years, however, both Hart and Parr completely withdrew from the company, leaving Ellis to operate the business until 1929, when Oliver acquired the tractor maker.

Twin City tractors came about by distilling a complex brew of industrialists. Philip Herzog went into business making fences in 1869. In 1882, he incorporated, and five years later, he took a partner renaming the company Gillette-Herzog. American Bridge Company purchased Gillette-Herzog in 1890, but in 1902, US Steel purchased American Bridge in what must have been an early day hostile takeover. The officers of American Bridge protected their interests by forming Minneapolis Malleable Iron two years earlier, and this concern formed one

leg supporting Minneapolis Steel & Machinery. The other leg, more easily seen, was Twin City Iron Works.

Twin City Iron Works was founded in 1889. Heavy steel and iron construction and fabrications were its business, but by 1903, the company was renamed Minneapolis Steel and began producing industrial steam engines. Shortly afterwards, it started manufacturing a German-made gas engine. This technology enabled it to produce tractors for J. I. Case Threshing Machine. It also began to build engines for Reeves & Company of Columbus, Indiana, for its 40 hp tractor. Reeves was bought during this time by Emerson-Brantingham, and Minneapolis Steel continued to produce the engine for that firm. Tractor production expanded even further when Bull Tractor Company, located in Minneapolis, arranged to have 4,600 Little Bull and Big Bull tractors built by Minneapolis Steel.

The company's own first tractor was in fact built outside its works. Five prototypes proved satisfactory, and Joy-Willson Company ultimately produced several hundred Twin City Model 40 tractors through 1920. Rated at 40-65 hp, it even offered a limited run of crawlers similar to and in competition with the Northern Holt Company's crawlers with front steering wheels, of eight years earlier. Twin City introduced a larger 60-90 hp model and a smaller 25-45 model at the same time.

As C. H. Wendel pointed out, with Joy-Willson building Twin City's tractors and Twin City building Bull's tractors, some conflict of direction must have occurred. Bull emphasized the value of smaller tractors even as Twin City was marketing bigger, heavier machines. For 1916 production, Minneapolis Steel sent Bull elsewhere to have its machines built.

By 1918, Minneapolis Steel had its own smaller tractors and introduced the Twin City 16-30, which it advertised as being automobile-like in style and engineering. Its exaggerated length, emphasized by its fully enclosed engine and sides, looked as rakish as that of many sports cars on the market. The tractor's overall length shortened in the next few years.

Minneapolis Steel, a manufacturer with considerable experience by this time, introduced its 12-20 Twin City in 1919, offering its four-cylinder engine with dual camshafts and four valves per cylinder. These remarkable improvements only recently have been rediscov-

The Big Steel Farmer

Just one look at this machine is enough to convince that here is a leader of Gas Tractors. It is the Steel combination of 40 horses and 20 men every working day—and in the only real power tests —in the month after month working tests—in the tests where all others have failed, we only ask the opportunity to show you that the Tractor of all Tractors has proven to be the

Twin City Tractor

Built in Two Sizes
25 Tractive H. P. and 40 Tractive H. P.

These Tractors have some wonderful records of things accomplished. Get the facts about scores of these machines in operation in every northwestern state—in Canada—down through Kansas—Texas—Mexico—Cuba—South America.

Let us send you a little booklet telling what other people did with the Twin City in 1912 alone, and another that tells just how the machine is made.

Write Today for our free books Nos. 15 and 17

Minneapolis Steel & Machinery Co.
Minneapolis, Minn.

We also conduct a school for Tractor Operators.

The Twin City Tractor was created by Minneapolis Steel & Machinery and continued in the Minneapolis-Moline line when that firm was formed from a three-way merger. The big gas engine could be had in either 25 or 40 hp versions in 1914.

ered for production passenger automobiles. By 1927, the 12-20 was putting out 17-28 hp with its twin-cam sixteen-valve engines.

In 1929, Minneapolis Steel joined Moline Plow and Minneapolis Threshing Company to create Minneapolis-Moline Power Implement Company.

The roots of the Minneapolis Threshing Machine are in Fond du Lac, Wisconsin, on the southern tip of Lake Winnebago, nearly 300 miles east of Minneapolis. John McDonald, a major backer of the threshing company founded in Fond du Lac in 1874, renamed the company after himself when financial troubles required reorganization only two years later. In 1887, with two successful machines behind him, he packed up and moved to Minneapolis.

McDonald's threshing machine was called the Pride of the West, and it was the first product of his newly organized Minneapolis Threshing Machine Company. He added a tractor line as well, and Minneapolis Threshing sold steam

tractors from the Huber line, from Marion, Ohio. Profiting from Edward Huber's patented innovations, McDonald entered the fray himself with his first steam traction engine offered in 1889.

McDonald soon investigated gasoline power. Two years of start-up expenses coupled with the gasoline experimentation must have contributed to McDonald's downfall, because in 1899, he lost control of his company.

McDonald's successor was much shrewder. Fred Kenaston, a Minneapolis banker and successful real estate speculator, bought John A. Abell Engine & Machinery Works in Toronto in order to gain entree into the Canadian markets. Then Kenaston acquired the Battle Creek, Michigan, Advance Thresher and formed the three companies into the American Abell Engine & Thresher Company. Although this operation cost more money than it earned, when Meinrad Rumely purchased Advance Thresher in 1911 from Minneapolis Threshing, part of the deal took American Abell. And that net result was a profit.

Gasoline tractors were less of a business risk by this time, and Kenaston and Minneapolis Threshing plunged again. In 1911, they agreed to distribute the 18 hp Universal Tractor made in Stillwater, Minnesota. Universal had been taken over by Northwest Thresher by this time, and the tractor, based on a design by A. O. Espe, was essentially their own. But when Rumely bought Northwest, it was marketed as the GasPull, and it was only available to Minneapolis Threshing for a short while longer, through 1912.

In 1911, an outside engineer, Walter McVicker, was hired to design a new machine to be assembled at Universal. The first, assembled through McVicker's own sources, was called the Minneapolis Farm Motor. Minneapolis Threshing brought the design in-house and made several changes including redesigning the radiator. Production began in 1912.

Rating 25-50 hp, the McVicker design was joined by a large 40-80 model, introduced in 1912. Both machines reflected Minneapolis Threshing's steam traction line-up. When Northwest Thresher could no longer accommodate Minneapolis Threshing's production demands, the 25-50 was dropped, and in 1914, a 20-40 bearing a strong family resemblance was introduced. Still big machines, the gasoline engine tractors sold nowhere near as successfully as

The Moline Universal Model D was tested at the University of Nebraska in mid-July 1920. Weighing 3,590 lb., Moline rated it as a 9–18 hp tractor but it produced more than 17 drawbar hp and more than 27 pulley hp. Below, this is a Moline two-bottom 14 in. plow.

Minneapolis Threshing's steamers. The company listed steamers in its catalog until 1923; by the end of production that year, it had sold nearly 8,000.

Philip Rose, General Motor's consulting engineer, visited Minneapolis Threshing in 1915. Kenaston impressed him: "About five years ago he added a gas tractor to his line of threshing machinery. It was all of that day a large heavy powerful machine adapted to breaking new land in the Northwest. The designer of this machine was W. J. McVicker . . . a thoroughly well trained engineer who has had considerable experience with gas engines and who has designed tractors for a number of concerns.

"I am told that the Minneapolis Threshing Machine Company are now considering the building of a small tractor. . . . It will probably make its appearance next spring. This company is always conservative and never plunges. Mr. Kenaston never makes a move until he sees where he is going to land. He had made money in the threshing machine business when others

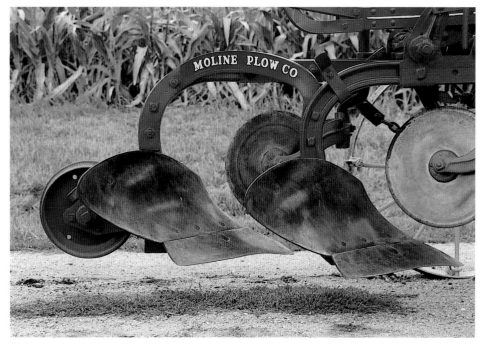

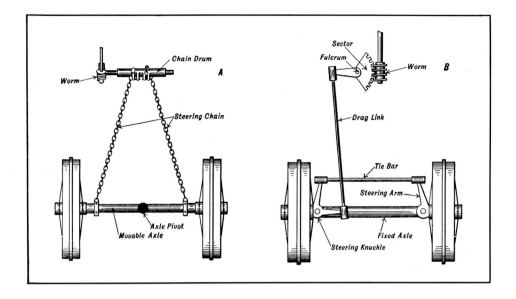

The Universal's steering gear swiveled the entire front-end engine assembly left or right and the plows trailed along behind. Top, these were the two tractor steering systems in use at the time.

have lost because he never loses his head. Besides this business is not his principal activity."

Rose was right. Kenaston introduced his All-Purpose 15-30 at the end of 1915. It resembled John Froelich's Waterloo Boy tractor, being set on a heavy channel-rail frame, with a transverse fan and offset steering. But the Minneapolis 15 used a vertical four-cylinder engine compared with Froelich's horizontal twin.

By 1920, the 15-30 had been tested and reclassified as 12-25 hp, and the massive 40-80 had been changed to 35-70. A smaller tractor, the Minneapolis 17-30, with a transverse-mounted upright four-cylinder engine appeared in 1922. This was supplemented in 1926 with the 17-30 Model B with a slightly longer wheelbase, when the 12-25 was discontinued. Both the 35-70 and 17-30 were produced until the company was absorbed along with Minneapolis Steel & Machinery and Moline Plow in 1929.

The Moline Plow Company was formed in 1870, the result of observant study of the farm implement business by two partners, Robert Swan and Henry Candee. Swan and Candee purchased a manufacturing operation back in 1852 in Moline, Illinois. Because of the success of several other Moline-area plow makers, the two induced Andrew Friberg to join their firm. As a plow maker, he was offered a partner's share for his experience. Another critical element, working capital, came from George Stephens, an automobile maker, and two other partners. Moline Plow was in business, and its logo, the Flying Dutchman, adopted in 1884, took off.

The next two decades witnessed a careful, reasoned period of acquisition. From the start, having its own steel company seemed advantageous, the only way to ensure the quality it sought. In 1904, it bought Acme Steel of Chicago.

Moline Plow added wagons and carriages in 1906, seed drills in 1909 and harvesters in 1913. Still, tractors, a growing market piece, were missing. International Harvester built five Moline Plow-designed prototypes in 1913, but the machine failed and none was manufactured.

The Universal Tractor Manufacturing Company was an offshoot of Ohio Carriage Manufacturing in Columbus, Ohio. Ohio Carriage had employed J. B. Funk, a tractor designer from Newcastle, Indiana, to produce a prototype small tractor for it in 1914. The Universal worked well enough in tests that Ohio Carriage's president H. C. Phelps founded a new company, Universal, while using Ohio Carriage to build the machines. Through 1915, it had sold 450, at $385. The Universal used a Reliable two-cylinder engine and was conceived more as a motor cultivator than as a tractor.

In November 1915, Moline Plow bought Universal, prior to its introduction of the Model D, a larger machine with a four-cylinder. The two-cylinder Universal continued in production un-

The Universal first appeared in 1914 from a Columbus, Ohio, company and sold for about $385. By the end of 1915, the company had sold to Moline Plow in Illinois. Below, its four-cylinder 3.50x5.00 in. engine was fitted with an electric governor, starter and headlight as standard equipment. The front wheel concrete ballasts came from the factory to reduce its tendency to tip. With its engine placed so high, a tight turn on even a slight hill invited frightening sensations. Below left, Jim Jonas, center, and his father George and uncle Frank, put finishing touches on Jim's 1919 Universal Model D. This tractor was difficult to drive; Jonas knew early owners who, on the first day they owned it, flipped a coin to see who would drive it. The loser drove the horses. The second day, the loser drove the Universal.

153

The 1920 Hart-Parr Model 30, owned by Eric Spitznogle of Wapello, Iowa, sold originally for $1,395. Below, introduced in 1918, the Model 30 was the first of Hart-Parr's small tractors. Tested in 1920 at the University of Nebraska, the 30 weighed in at 5,450 lb.

til 1917 when the D was offered, now with a Moline Plow-built engine. The next year, American farmers who bought the Universal got the first tractor offered with electric self-starter and a headlight as standard equipment.

All of Stephens' automobile interests had come with him into Moline Plow over the years. John Willys, manufacturer of the Willys-Overland automobiles became interested. That interest led to Willys' acquisition of major controlling interest in Moline Plow.

In 1919, Moline Plow acquired Independent Harvester Company, and in 1921, the engineering consulting firm of Root & Vandervoort was added to Moline Plow's organization. In 1922, as Stephens' auto company introduced its Salient Six, a luxurious touring car, Moline Plow was beginning to suffer from the post World War I recession. By 1923, Willys picked up Stephens' auto lines for his Overland production and dropped manufacture of the Universal Motor Plow. For the next six years, Moline Plow limited its line while struggling to stay afloat. In mid-May 1929, the company joined two others to form Minneapolis-Moline Power Implement.

Born in 1929, Minneapolis-Moline Power Implement Company was the offspring of Minneapolis Steel & Machinery, Minneapolis Threshing Machine and Moline Implement. The infant Minneapolis-Moline Power Implement took profit from the hard times that befell its competitors. It is likely that the worldwide economic depression that broke so many competitors might well have done those parents in had they not merged.

The new conglomerate reflected common merger practice, as existing inventories were exhausted. The Twin City tractors of the Minneapolis Threshing Machine line continued until 1931 when M-M introduced its own machine. The Twin City 17-28 three-plow tractor, the 17-30 Model B and the five-plow 27-44 were joined by a 21-32. With well-engineered, thoroughly tested and fully developed machines, the

Steering the Model 30 used an automotive-type system. Its top speed was slightly less than 3 mph. Left, the 30 was powered by Hart-Parr's own cross-mounted horizontal two-cylinder 6.50x7.00 in. engine. Nebraska tests rated nearly 20 drawbar hp, and 31.3 hp on the pulley.

155

Twin City line was highly regarded. Its water pumps, variable fuel carburetion, dual-system air cleaners and pressure oil lubrication pumps led Minneapolis-Moline to advertise the machines' long life: "Three Extra Years is the Reputation of All Twin City Tractors."

In 1930, M-M introduced its Kombination Tractor (KT), an 11–20 hp rated machine. The KT was so named because of the combination of tasks for which it was suited: its standard tread design managed the plow, the cultivator, the farm wagon or drive belt work, or could operate implements driven by the optional PTO. Over the years, the KT appeared in an orchard version; the replacement KTA appeared in 1934.

Minneapolis-Moline brought out its own completely original design in 1931, when it introduced the Universal Model (M), a row crop general-purpose wide-tread tricycle. A complete line of implements ensured its usefulness. In early 1934, M-M introduced the new Universal and the Standard Model J. Both used an F-head engine—intake above, exhaust below—to prolong valve life and increase power from its four-cylinder engines. Orchard models were continued with the J. The Model MTA replaced the earlier M.

Minneapolis-Moline engineers continued engine innovations and announced the Model Z in late 1936. Engine compression could be adjusted by exchanging the heads. This flexibility also aided engine valvetrain service. The earlier Model U was supplemented with a new GT five-plow standard tractor and with the Model R compact tractor.

By 1938, styling was prevalent in the industry and bright colors were necessary to sell tractors. To introduce its new Prairie Gold tractors, M-M showed off its new styled machinery at the home office to some 12,000 invited guests. The striking Model U-DLX (U-deluxe) was joined by a line-up of Visionlined tractors, and the show startled the visitors.

The company had conceived the U-DLX Comfortractor as a dual-purpose machine to work the farm and combat the automobile. With its fully enclosed cab and its strong resemblance to the cars of the day, it was imagined the farmer could work the field all day and then, in fifth gear at 40 mph, take the wife into town for the church social in the same machine. But it was pricey—$1,900 at introduction; nearly $1,000 more than the cost of a standard U and a bit ostentatious for some farmers. Complete with a heater and radio, the U-DLX made most farmers feel a greater sense of accomplishment while they worked in entertained comfort next to their neighbor freezing or clouded in dust. Something like 150 sold, and many of those were used year round.

The U Series of tractors led to another M-M innovation and the creation of another legendary machine. Introduced in late 1938, the UTX tractor was an all-wheel-drive machine for the military which was first tested by the Minnesota

Orchard tractors were fully enclosed, more for the protection of fragile trees and produce than for the engine and driver convenience. Yet in 1937 the streamline era was in full force and even the practical farm tractor took on stylish sheet metal to advance its function. Left, Minneapolis-Moline's Twin City Model J was offered from 1936 through 1938. The J was capable of as much as 12 mph. Far left, power for the J came from Minneapolis-Moline's 3.625x4.750 in. four-cylinder engine.

National Guard. This conversion was produced during World War II, and came to be known as the Jeep. Jeep was a regular character in the Popeye The Sailorman cartoons who could do anything and knew everything. The U conversions fit the bill and a Guardsman at Camp Ripley nicknamed one of the first ones. The name stuck. Thousands were built.

The Jeep was built from the Comfortractor cab and rear end. M-M used their 425 ci six-cylinder engine and added front-wheel drive to make a four-wheel-drive machine. A roller replaced the front bumper to climb over obstacles or push down trees.

The rounded front end resulted from many styling changes. The last versions of the Jeep used M-M's Z engine with hydraulic valve lifters. Versions of the ZTS and ZASM were produced for the US Air Force and the Army Corps of Engineers as industrial utility vehicles up to 1953. However, M-M continued to produce utility tractors for the military through the late 1950s.

LPG was introduced as a fuel option in 1941, making M-M the first to take advantage of the inexpensive fuel as a power source. Two years later, a smaller sibling of the U-DLX was

---

Gary & Lyle Spitznogle:

Still the Old Reliable

Gnats swarm ferociously, unrelentingly. It rained last night, and Gary and Lyle Spitznogle's farm needs no farm dog. The gnats will drive off the most determined visitor.

"Out in the wind, these little things ain't no problem," Lyle recalls. "'Course, there ain't no wind," he says, arms fluttering furiously.

There is not exactly *no* wind. The treetops 30 ft. above the lane are getting blasted senseless—but only very locally and only about twice every five or six seconds.

"It's a hit and miss system," Gary explains. "And when there's no load on it, it just barely runs." The engine hits again. Two quick reports. It sounds like a high school marching band drummer blasting double snare drum rim shots in a medium-pace John Philip Sousa march.

The noise that occurs during the "miss" cycle is harder to define.

"That's the camshaft and the drive pulley going around. They're exposed and that's what you hear," Gary solves the mystery but doesn't describe the noise.

Swirl a handful of ball bearings inside a galvanized pail. That describes the noise.

Swirl. Swirl. Swirl. Double rim shot. Swirl. Swirl.

And with each double rim shot, the trees 30 ft. above the top of the stack blow wildly.

There are no gnats up there.

History generally credits Gary's 1913 Hart-Parr with being the first commercially successful farm tractor. In fact, it came to be known as Old Reliable.

It looks more put together than assembled. It is a collection of geometrics, the assortment of which came from an illustrator's basic template of simple shapes.

Seen from behind as it moves up the lane, it gives new perspective to the ease with which farmers plant and cultivate and harvest nearly a century after this Old Reliable scored the earth. It requires a busy collection of activities. Gary appears constantly occupied with cranking the steering wheel in gross turns to accomplish minor course corrections. Driving it is not difficult, only challenging. Like the gnats.

Neither is starting it difficult. Like the gnats, it is only challenging: First, retard the timing. Second, open the compression release valves on both cylinders. Third, turn the fuel on. Fourth, turn the switch to batteries (in earlier times, one switched on the magneto). Fifth, turn the flywheel over until it starts. Sixth, once it has started, come back around and close the compression release valves. Seventh, advance the timing. Eighth, throw the traction key in on the belt pulley. Ninth, throw the clutch forward to go forward, or pull back to reverse; Old Reliable has only one speed in each direction. Tenth, drive away.

Simple enough. Of course, the starting procedure gains in stature with the knowledge that the flywheel itself weighs 840 lb., and that connected as it is to the crankshaft and two pistons, you must turn over nearly 3,000 lb.

The entire machine weighs just less than 20,000 lb. Its two-cylinder engine, measuring 10x15 in. bore and stroke, produced 30 hp at the drawbar at an almost countable 300 rpm. Old Reliable did not accelerate. It gathered speed. To a sedate 2.3 mph.

It dispatched gnats much quicker.

The 1937 Minneapolis-Moline Twin City Model JT Orchard is owned by Walter and Bruce Keller of Kaukauna, Wisconsin.

built in limited numbers for the military. A cab was fitted to the little Model R.

For the early 1950s, Minneapolis-Moline continued to offer its tried and true Model U, while introducing diesel engines. The row crop U was supplemented with a Model S standard tread, a Model N single front tire with wide rear tread and a Model E with adjustable front-tread width. Disc brakes were standard. High-crop cane modifications, available since the late 1940s, were continued for the Model U as well. A power boost system, Ampli-torq—basically a dual-range transmission—was introduced and halved ground speed while increasing its drawbar pull. The Uni-Tractor was introduced as well; called the Model L, it was essentially designed as a power platform to operate various harvest implements. At the same time, M-M picked up the tractor lines manufactured by B. F. Avery and offered Avery's V, BF and BG tractors through 1955 when the last tractors were phased out.

In its introductory brochure, Minneapolis-Moline published a survey explaining that 50 percent of the farmers wanted a tractor with a cab. Minneapolis-Moline responded with its U-DLX, putting a bi-fold door at the rear to open to full cab width and including roll-up windows, windshield wipers, a heater and a radio. Left, the Model U-DLX could be purchased without the cab, but with a cab it competed with the automobile.

Aggressive new looks identified the 445 model line, introduced in the late 1950s. Running on LPG, diesel or gasoline, the model boasted slightly increased power to go with its new appearance.

Then in 1969, Minneapolis-Moline was itself phased out, acquired along with Oliver Farm Equipment and Cockshutt Farm Equipment of Canada to become the farm equipment division of White. Forty years after three competitors merged to stave off financial disaster and economic ruin, farm implement history was exactly duplicating itself. This time, Minneapolis-Moline, Oliver and Cockshutt, hobbled by overproduc-

tion and sagging farm incomes, combined to do the same—to pool resources, eliminate duplication, concentrate production . . . and stay in business.

The chilled plow was perfected in a process invented by James Oliver in 1855. Oliver cooled the freshly cast iron with a stream of water. During his process, he annealed, or glazed, the plowing surface to polish it and make it resistant to rust while improving its ability to scour. The slow, water-bath cooling enhanced the strength of the iron without making it brittle.

Soon after perfecting the process, Oliver protected it with patents.

It was another thirteen years, before his success required incorporation to protect his business, in 1868. The Scotsman settled in South Bend, Indiana, east of Chicago, and founded the South Bend Iron Works. The company produced plows and marketed and developed other farm implements. By 1898, the Oliver Chilled Plow Works had grown to the point that the US government was looking into antitrust proceedings, accusing Oliver Chilled Plow, as well as Deere, Case and others, of price fixing. Oliver Chilled Plow, still not a large company by 1920, was startled to learn that Henry Ford was planning to sell hundreds of thousands of Fordson tractors with Oliver plows as part of the price.

In the spring of 1929, even as Minneapolis-Moline was coming together in the Twin Cities, Oliver Farm Equipment Company was being forged out of the assembly of James Oliver's Chilled Plow, Hart-Parr, Nichols & Shepard and American Seeding Machine Company. For Oli-

The 1939 Minneapolis-Moline Model U-DLX was also known as the Comfortractor. It was the earliest attempt to bring creature comforts to the farmer. With its enclosed cab, heater and radio, the farmer enjoyed protection from the elements his neighbors still faced. Left, M-M introduced high-compression engines to farming in 1935. While the competition still offered 4.0:1 and 4.1:1 engines, M-M produced more power and better fuel efficiency with 5.25:1 engines. Roger Mohr's father sold M-M implements and tractors during the late 1930s and Mohr remembered riding in a Comfortractor. The memory triggered his collection, of which this 1939 U-DLX is a part.

Dale Gerken's 1948 Minneapolis-Moline Model U stands almost camouflaged against fall corn in Fort Dodge, Iowa. M-M called their flaxen color Prairie Gold and all M-M tractors after the late 1930s brightened up considerably over the former gray with red trim. Below, the Model U was powered by M-M's own four-cylinder 4.25x5.00 in. engine. It produced 26.8 hp at the drawbar, and 33.4 hp on the belt pulley. It sold for slightly less than $1,800.

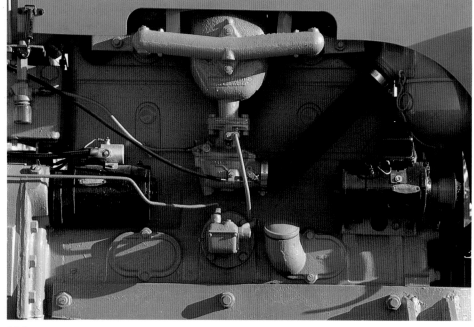

ver, it was expansion into the major leagues. It went far beyond the Sherman Commission antitrust accusations because, if anything, it now made Oliver much more competitive.

The new Oliver had four separate divisions: the former Oliver represented just the plow and tillage equipment portion of the full-line company, Nichols & Shepard contributed its Red River Special threshers, Superior Seeding endowed the new company with its seed planting and fertilizing machinery, and the firm's Hart-Parr division manufactured and marketed tractors under the name Oliver Hart-Parr.

The first Oliver Hart-Parr was introduced in 1930, the 18–28, with an upright, longitudinally mounted four-cylinder engine. Orchard and rice-field versions were offered, and in 1931, an industrial version was added. Hart-Parr quickly adopted rubber tires, and in 1932, pneumatic tires replaced the hard rubber.

A slightly different engine configuration powered the row-crop 18–27 introduced in

1930. Hart-Parr also introduced its spider-web-like "tiptoe" steel wheels. Then in 1935, Oliver Hart-Parr introduced its styled and stylish Model 70.

As Oliver's Hart-Parr Division public relations crowed, "In automobiles, streamlines have followed the development of high compression motors; new beauty symbolized new, smooth power. Related to the automobile (by an early marriage to internal combustion) farm tractors now boast both high compression power and streamlined beauty since the Oliver Company put the first six-cylinder tractor on a production basis, calling it the Oliver '70.'"

The 70, urged into production by Oliver president M. W. Ellis (formerly Hart-Parr president), used a small-displacement automobile-type six-cylinder engine. The 70 HC (high compression) was designed to be used with standard 70 octane pump gasoline, whereas a 70 KD was meant for use with kerosene or distillates. Steering brakes provided an 8 ft. turning radius. All the engine and implement controls were within finger reach of the automobile-style steering wheel.

A 1915 ad from an early power farming journal for the Oliver Marsh Engine teamed up with the Oliver Chilled Plow Works' gang plow.

But the tractor's clean bodywork was most striking. Its raked-back grille was crowned with the Oliver Hart-Parr logo, though by this time, the Oliver name was larger, reversing the trend on previous models. Electric lights, starter and battery were optional, though by 1938, these were included. Standard and orchard versions adopted the same stylish appearance.

Oliver got the farmer involved in marketing its new tractors, by sponsoring a color contest at state fairs. The object was for the farmers to vote on the new tractor's official color combination, and tractors painted in all the candidate colors were displayed—and sold—around the United States. The winner? Meadow Green with Clover White trim.

Oliver's companion models did not get the designer's fine touch at first. The 1937 Model 90 standard resembled its Hart-Parr lineage. In 1938, the Model 80 followed the 90's conservative lines, in both row-crop and standard configurations. A diesel 80 was introduced in 1940.

The year 1940 also brought out the Oliver Model 60, another in the Model 70 Fleetline mold. It was produced through 1948 when all the previous tractors were replaced by the Fleetline 66, 77 and 88 tractors. Hydra-Lectric onboard hydraulics provided Oliver's version of the Ferguson Draft Control system. These remained in production until their replacements in 1954, the Super Series.

Super tractors ran from 55 through 99, upgrading the three previous models as well. Oliver's Hydra-Lectric system was retained, and

a three-point hitch was optional; the patents on Harry Ferguson's system had run out. Independent PTO was acquired from the Cockshutt line. The design of the Super series reflected comparable styles of the 1950s; the louvered panels covering the engine disappeared, showing off the functional workings. The horizontal-slash grille looked aggressive and powerful.

In 1959, all the tractor model designations multiplied by ten and the grilles became egg-crates for an even more businesslike, competent appearance. The corporate colors continued, including the model numbers in a slash along the side. A torque converter Power Booster drive was offered on 770 and 880 Series tractors, reducing speed to increase pull. A Lugmatic torque converter for the 990 automatically selected the engine range needed to produce adequate torque for the load. With the standard six-speed transmission, a one-third increase in torque was available.

In 1960, Oliver celebrated the twenty-fifth anniversary of its six-cylinder engines. Its development had taken a 201 ci six-cylinder with a 6.5:1 compression ratio producing 28 hp at 1500 rpm and increased it to a 265 ci six-cylinder with an 8.5:1 compression ratio producing 76 hp at 2000 rpm. Within days of the celebration, Oliver Farm Equipment announced its acquisition by White Motor Corporation of Cleveland.

In 1962, the Oliver Division of White purchased Cockshutt Farm Equipment of Canada. In 1969, when White acquired Minneapolis-

The Oliver 70, far left, was available in standard, row crop and orchard configurations. For collector John Jonas of Wahoo, Nebraska, this standard version was rarer than the row crop versions used more frequently in the Midwest. Left, the Cockshutt Model 30 was tested at the University of Nebraska over Memorial Day 1947. Using the Buda 3.430x4.125 in. four-cylinder engine, in fourth gear it could run 10 mph at 1,650 rpm. Below, the engine produced 21.68 hp at the drawbar, and 30.28 hp on the pulley. Cockshutt introduced the continuous-running power takeoff, which kept power to accessories even when forward motion was stopped.

Moline, a new company was spun off. White Farm Equipment was founded. The massive merger over the 1960s brought together the ideas and patents, the experiments and profits of four dozen farm machinery and implement manufacturers. It consolidated more than 150 years of history under one corporate roof.

Oliver brought expertise in seeding and fertilizing tools. It added the success of its fuel-efficient and high-powered tractors. In two- and four-wheel drive, the legacy of its fifteen companies drove the organization right up to 1960.

Cockshutt and its multiple mergers brought specialization in harvesting equipment and innovative medium-horsepower tractors. This came as the result of the blending of nearly one dozen Canadian firms, which culminated in 1962.

Minneapolis-Moline brought an alphabet soup of contributors in as many fields as there are fields. From its threshers to its plows to its tractors, Minneapolis-Moline absorbed the best

Cockshutt of Brantford, Ontario, marketed the Model 30 in the United States as the National Farm Equipment Co-Op E–3. Cockshutt was the first tractor manufactured in Canada to be tested by the Nebraska test facility. Below, the Cockshutt was sold on 11x38 in. rear tires and 5.50x16 in. fronts. During its Nebraska tests, the 3,609 lb. tractor pulled 2,122 lb. By 1950, Cockshutt introduced the six-cylinder Buda and renamed the tractor as the Model 40.

of two dozen organizations before it reached 1969.

History, especially farm equipment history, repeats itself. We learn from history and profit from our mistakes.

But we cannot control the weather and we cannot predict the world politics, which both conspire to affect the climate of business and the profit to the farmer. So it is not surprising that in December 1980, Texas Investment Corporation acquired the White Farm Equipment Company—meaning all four dozen of its predecessors—and operated it as a subsidiary, still under White's name.

And it is then no more surprising that in November 1985, Allied Products Corporation acquired some of the assets of the White Farm Equipment Division of Texas Investment—

meaning some of the four dozen of its predecessors. Allied already owned New Idea Farm Equipment Corporation.

So it was predictable that in May 1987, the White Division and New Idea Division would merge. The new company was called White-New Idea Farm Equipment Company.

It is lastly comforting to know that in 1991, with the history of fifty companies involved, White tractor manufacture continued at the Charles City plant, home of one of its predecessors for nearly a century.

A father and son hobby, Jeff Gravert restored the 1947 Cockshutt Model 30, under the watchful eye of his father, Carroll. Heartland Automotive, in Central City, Nebraska, is Carroll's restoration shop.

Chapter 10

The Orphan Tractors

The idea of selling tractors spurred Durant's imagination. He had ideas of revolutionizing the business of selling farm implements.
Lawrence R. Gustin, *Billy Durant—Creator of General Motors*, 1973

For all the tractor makers absorbed or acquired by the surviving major producers, many more simply went out of business. In some cases, these manufacturers of orphan tractors produced only one model for a year or two, such as Graham-Bradley and its Model 32. Or they survived decades of success with other products and then failed to survive a technology change-over, such as Russell & Company.

The orphans discussed here represent the products of major national firms and minor local ones. They are the results of manufactured products lacking quality and of quality manufacturers lacking products.

The H. W. Rice portable steam engine, built in 1884, was a scratch-tube boiler that burned the fire in back; the heat rose, turned back and went out the stack. A California machine, constructed in San Francisco, the Rice was meant to burn straw; wood and coal were precious commodities in the central valleys of the state.

Rice started in 1864 in steam development. Many of the early California steamers placed the engine on the side of the boiler. Because of side-hill planting and harvesting, when these engines were pulled by horses, the likelihood of tipping was great. It was Rice's innovation to put the engine up on top.

Thaddeus Fairbanks perfected a scale that ensured an accurate record of weight in 1830.

Twenty years later, in 1850, a young St. Johnsbury, Vermont, resident applied for work with Fairbanks. He was seventeen and his name was Charles H. Morse. He signed on for three years at $50 per year with the avowed ambition of learning all there was to know about scales.

As Fairbanks, Morse & Company said in its own company history *Pioneers in Industry—1830–1945*, "The Fairbanks scale was already an established product when Charles Hosmer Morse arrived at maturity. But he recognized the epoch-making commercial possibilities of other inventions . . . long before most people did, and had the courage and faith to invest his time, energy and money in developing and perfecting them."

Orphans for adoption; tractors without parents or offspring. The 1938 Graham-Bradley was such a machine. Built by an automobile manufacturer and sold only through a mail-order catalog retailer, it was an industrial life waiting for extinction.

The 1884 H. W. Rice portable steam engine normally operated at 110 lb. pressure. Still getting regular use by the Agricultural Machinery Collection of the University of California at Davis, the Rice is now limited to 60 lb. boiler pressure, far left. At left, two flywheels flank the operator's seat. The Rice was horse-drawn from one work site to the next. Below, the ball governor sits atop the steam chest which houses the slide valve. The valve coming off the top is the main steam valve out of the dome. In the upper left hand corner are two pressure-release valves sitting on top of the dome. The original valve is on the right and is supplemented by a newer version next to it.

Five years later, Morse was promoted to partner. Fairbanks, Morse & Company. expanded quickly after that, acquiring the Williams Engine Works in Beloit, Wisconsin, which made steam engines.

By 1893, Morse had learned of the gasoline engines of James Charter and his father, John. Morse convinced James to come to work at Beloit to head the gas engine works there. Within the same year, James shipped out the first four-cycle gasoline engine. The Jack-of-All-Trades engine was perfected for the farm and became the most popular, reliable form of power available.

Fairbanks, Morse produced self-powered railroad crew cars, which used the company's small gasoline engines, and by 1910 had begun experimenting with farm tractors, adapting its larger stationary engines for traction uses. The first prototype used its 25 hp single-cylinder engine. A larger version, the 30-60, was introduced in 1912. It ran off a two-cylinder engine and weighed 14 tons.

Introduced in late 1912 for 1913 sales, the 15-25 was improved, and engine speed was

increased so that its output was raised as well, to 15-30 hp. Sales of the 8 ton tractor were especially good in Canada where its pulling ability was most used. Production of tractors ended in Beloit in 1914. Both were very heavy machines intended for Western breaking. They were designed by the general engineering staff.

Fairbanks, Morse went on to perfect and market gasoline and diesel stationary engines. Out of the business by 1918, it never returned.

Philip Rose, General Motor's industrial spy of 1915, summarized and dismissed the future of Russell & Company of Massillon, Ohio:

"These people are too slow for the gas tractor game. They are afraid to venture."

The past had been altogether different. Founded in 1842, the Russell brothers Charles, Nahum and Clement were carpenters who experimented with building a thresher. It succeeded, and C. M. Russell Company grew to be Massilon's biggest employer. It produced steam traction engines by the hundreds and railroad cars by the thousands.

Russell steam traction engines were characterized as simple and straightforward. They were available from 6 hp up to monster 150 hp "road locomotives." The 150's weight must have been incredible because it used its own steam power to assist steering. The 150s were marketed before 1910, though Russell continued steam traction engines through the mid-1920s.

In 1909, Russell introduced its first gasoline engine. It was basically a steam traction chassis fitted with a gasoline engine because the machine produced 22-44 hp and yet weighed nearly 9 tons. Called the American, it tested at the Winnipeg Tractor trials in 1909. The American was a tricycle, and this reappeared in a 1911–1913 production 30-60 hp 12 tonner.

Introduced in 1913, the 30-60 four-wheeler also was based on Russell's steam traction engine technology. It used a transverse-mounted four-cylinder engine. It was in production only a short while, replaced by the Russell Giant, which was introduced as a 40-80 but which tests forced to be rerated at 30-60 hp. Weighing 12 tons, it used a transverse four of 8x10 inch dimensions: everything about the Giant was gigantic. The model was offered in Russell's line until 1927.

In 1915, Russell introduced its lighter tractors, the 12-24 weighing only 4,650 lb. Called the

HACKNEY AUTO PLOW

This Rice portable engine was fired with straw, wood being too scarce a commodity in central California. The 18 hp engine probably sold for around $1,800. On the other end of the spectrum was the Hackney Auto Plow, above. The Hackney Brothers, Leslie, William and Joseph, produced tricycle-style tractors from 1909 until fire destroyed their last factory in St. Paul, Minnesota, in January 1918.

177

The 1911 Fairbanks, Morse Model 15–25 weighed about 16,000 lb. This rare tractor was restored and is maintained by the Antique Gas and Steam Engine Museum at Vista, California. Below, while the big flywheel turned at 250 rpm, the screen cooler at the front of the tractor was fed by a centrifugal water pump, which was belt-driven. Right, oil feeds the main bearings and other internals of the Model 15–25. The glass reminded the farmer to be sure his engine was being lubricated. The engine was a huge horizontal single, 10.5 in. bore and 18 in. stroke for total displacement 1557 ci. Far right, a 1911 ad for Fairbanks, Morse.

Russell Jr., it was supplemented by the Little Boss 15-30 in 1917. The Big Boss was a 20-35 and, like all the smaller tractors, bore strong physical resemblance to the Lauson and Heider tractors with fully enclosed engines and operator cabins under canopies.

In March 1927, Russell & Company was sold at an auction, and no more tractors were produced. Rose wrote the epitaph for this company a dozen years early: "This is another of the old line thresher companies that has made a success of the threshing machine business. It has fooled with the tractor game for several years but never got far."

William Crapo Durant had founded General Motors in 1908, and as founder, he frequently got his way. An opportunity to purchase Ford Motor Company outright in 1909 for $8

million that was missed owing to banking squabbles left him smarting over anything Ford might attempt.

Durant was born in 1861 in Boston, the grandson of the governor of Michigan, Henry Crapo. After his grandfather's death, Durant's family moved back to the family home in Flint, Michigan.

On the spur of the moment, Durant borrowed $2,000 from family friends and bought a buggy business in 1886 after a ride had impressed him with the smoothness of the cart's suspension. The jump from horse carts to automobiles was simply a matter of time and financing.

And when his arch rival Henry Ford announced plans to introduce a small tractor, Durant's competitive nature surged.

Philip Rose visited eighty-one companies during 1915 in his consulting for General Motors, and his report, *The Black Book*, guided Durant in his purchase of Samson Iron Works of Stockton, California.

Rose thought highly of Samson: "Mr. Kroyer [J. M. Kroyer, president and general manager] was the real inventor, and various assistants work out the ideas. The small tractor is the only

The 1915 Russell 30–60 "Giant" was introduced as a 40–80 but in June 1921, when tested at the University of Nebraska, the results forced renumbering. This giant was restored and is part of the Agricultural Machinery Collection at the University of California at Davis.

one that they make now. They turn out about fifteen hundred tractors annually.... Mr. Kroyer is a practical business man and mechanic of the most matter of fact type. His technical assistant is a college man but like most college men—meaning no offense—he lacks the untrammeled initiative and creative ability of his employer who has no experience with anything but practical matters."

Samson's one small tractor was its 6–12 hp tricycle. The 6–12 ran a single-cylinder engine. Twins and four-cylinder engines were used in successive models. The tractor was a low-slung design setting the machinery between two wide-set, wide-tread rear wheels, which served to keep the center of gravity low and reduce the

chance of tipping on the hills around Stockton. Its open wheels, called the Sieve Grip, offered plenty of grip with virtually no compaction. The Model S 25 hp followed. But in 1917, its $1,750 price was more than double that of Ford's Fordson.

So Samson became a General Motors Corporation subsidiary, to be assembled in a plant specially purchased in Janesville, Wisconsin. And GM engineer Arthur Mason was assigned to design a new tractor for the new division. It resembled the Fordson, but did not appear quite so finished and was known as the Model M. Introduced in 1918, it sold for $650.

But Durant had an idea of his own, a tractor for the farmer who missed working behind

180

Steering was chain-and-bolster style, and ran 22 turns lock to lock. Levers control direction, gear selection and clutch. An almost useless foot brake is visible just below the seat.

A unique feature of the Russell engine was its hinge. The crankcase, held together by bolts, split in half and folded forward onto the manifolds for piston and crankshaft service. Far right, the dual ignition system used a low-tension system as well as a distributor-type coil (not visible). Running at 525 rpm, the L-head engine was capable of 3.2 mph in top gear. Below, the 23,380 lb. tractor produced 43.5 hp at the drawbar but only 66.1 hp off its pulley, running on kerosene. Russell fitted flywheels on both sides so dual belt operations were possible.

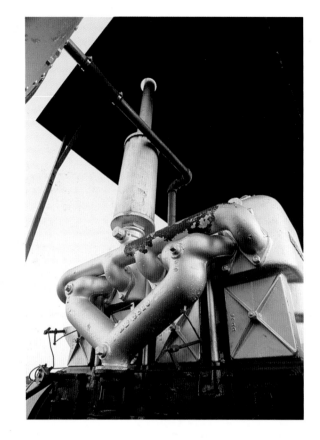

horses. Durant's new Samson would be gasoline powered and controlled by reins. Called the Iron Horse, the tractor was actually a renamed Jim Dandy Motor Cultivator and was generally a failure, being poorly balanced and difficult to operate. It was to sell for $450 in 1920.

"Samson was to be more than a tractor company," Ed Cray reported in his *Chrome Colossus—General Motors and Its Times* in 1980. "Durant envisioned it supplying farmers with all their tool needs—including farm implements..., electric lighting and appliances..., and finally two trucks and a nine-passenger family car. Farmers had large families and hired hands, all of whom wanted to go to church on Sunday, Durant piously explained."

By this time, nearly 1920, the economy was unwinding into the post World War I depression as European farmers recovered and US farm produce exports fell. And General Motors' backers were concerned at the cost Durant was incurring to develop tractors. In the end, it came to $33 million. In the end, in 1921, Samson was put out of its stockholders' misery.

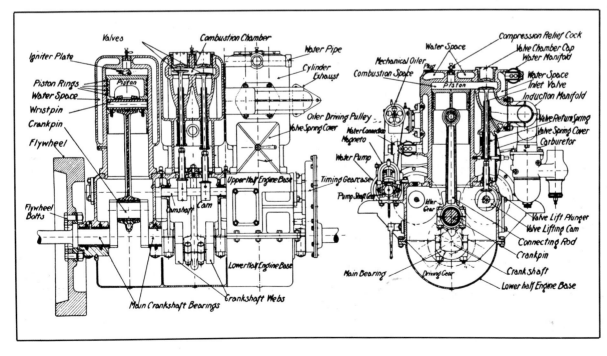

Valves
Combustion Chamber
Igniter Plate
Water Pipe
Cylinder Exhaust
Piston Rings
Piston
Water Space
Wristpin
Crankpin
Flywheel
Oiler Driving Pulley
Valve Spring Cover
Water Connection
Magneto
Water Pump
Upper Half Engine Base
Timing Gearcase
Pump Shaft Gear
Flywheel Bolts
Camshaft Cam
Idler Gear
Lower Half Engine Base
Water Space
Compression Relief Cock
Valve Chamber Cap
Water Manifold
Mechanical Oiler
Plug
Combustion Space
Piston
Water Space
Inlet Valve
Induction Manifold
Valve Return Spring
Valve Spring Cover
Carburetor
Valve Lift Plunger
Valve Lifting Cam
Connecting Rod
Crankpin
Crank shaft
Lower half Engine Base
Main Bearing
Driving Gear
Main Crankshaft Bearings
Crankshaft Webs

The crank side of the engine shows the crank hanging below the giant round radiator. The crank engages the lower shaft, which slides in to turn the crankshaft. Left, the first tractor Russell & Co., of Massillon, Ohio, offered was a British built machine. Introduced in 1909, it was called "The American," and featured a three-cylinder 8x10 in. engine. The L-head engine produced 22 hp at the drawbar.

Samson Iron Works of Stockton, California, came under careful scrutiny before General Motors purchased them. GM sent an independent engineer around the United States examining more than 90 other companies before recommending Samson to President Will Durant. GM bought Samson hoping to compete with Henry Ford and his Fordson. But its original selling price of $1,750 and its original appearance gave it two strokes against the cheaper competitors, far left. Below, Samson's wheels gripped far better than their open pattern would suggest. The spongy soil around Stockton led to the design, and the wheels became known as Sieve Grips because of their traction.

185

By 1918, GM owned Samson and puts its badging all over the low-slung machine. The four-cylinder 4.75x6.00 in. engine produced 12 hp at the drawbar and 25 hp on the pulley, and an indignant bark to the ear. Right, this Model S–25 weighed 5,000 lb. It is owned by Fred Heidrick of Woodland, California. Far right, the 1921 Union Sure Grip 12–25 hp Model D is reported to be the last one left. This unique California machine is part of the Agricultural Machinery Collection at the University of California at Davis.

The Union Tool Sure-Grip was produced by a toolmaker and foundry in Torrance, California. The Model D 12–25 was produced only in 1921 and 1922. Using its own four-cylinder engine, the crawler design bore some resemblance to Best's earlier 30 hp tractor, without the front steering wheels. The single front wheel of the Sure-Grip was only a free-spinning castor, the steering accomplished by steering clutches and brakes. Clearly nose heavy, the Sure-Grip

187

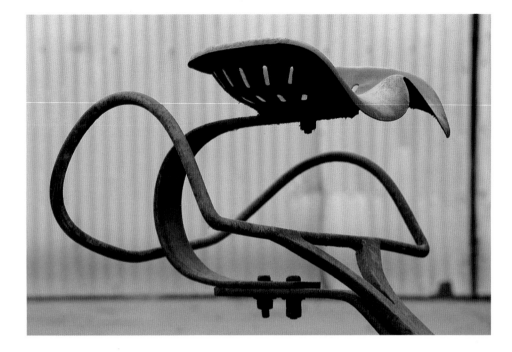

Referred to in polite company as a "rear guard," the hoop surrounding the operator's seat protected the farmer from falling or being struck by objects as he turned the Union tractor. The driver's position was cantilevered out behind the transmission. Far right, the Union's front castor wheel was only a support for the engine. Steering was accomplished by the crawler tracks using clutches and brakes. Right, there was no suspension on tractors so manufacturers gave suspension to the radiators to protect the copper tubes and soldered joints from constant impact. The UTCO insignia stands for the Union Tool Co. of Torrance, California.

needed its front wheel for balance. The tractor rated 8 drawbar horsepower.

Sears Roebuck & Company sold tractors for a few years, the Bradley General Purpose (GP) in 1931 and then the Graham-Bradley 32 hp in 1938 and 1939.

The Sears Bradley GP was a tricycle two-plow-rated machine that used a Waukesha four-cylinder engine. According to R. B. Gray's *The Agricultural Tractor—1855–1950*, the Bradley was among the first to offer variable tread width and direct PTO.

The Paige-Detroit Motor Car Company was founded in Detroit in 1908. For the next eigh-

The operator's legs straddled the transmission housing. Two levers operated brakes and the other two operated clutches. You needed four hands to drive, but your feet were just along for the ride. Below, valve lifters and rocker arms were exposed to the elements like most tractors of the period. Union Tool built its own engines.

The 1938 Graham-Bradley General Purpose tractor was built by the Graham-Paige Motors Corp. of Detroit, makers of sleek, fast and powerful automobiles. The Graham Brothers reputation for speed and style influenced their tractor efforts and their 20 hp, 20 mph tractor suggested much more of both. Right, many of the mechanical parts were interchangeable with Dodge truck parts of the period; the rear brakes are truck drums.

teen years, the Paige automobiles were mostly sporty roadsters with the occasional sedan tourer thrown in. In 1928, Joseph, Robert and Ray Graham acquired the Paige company and produced some striking, racy automobiles themselves.

The Graham brothers entered the tractor market using one of their smaller six-cylinder engines as power. The tractor came standard from Detroit with electric battery start and headlights, PTO, rubber tires and hydraulic lift. The Graham brothers' racing interests bled over into the tractor as well, for its four-speed transmission provided a top speed of 22 mph. The belt pulley was coupled through the transmission and offered four speeds plus reverse. Yet the

Dale Gerken of Fort Dodge, Iowa, owns this 1938 Graham-Bradley. Below, powered by Graham-Paige's Continental flathead stove-bolt six-cylinder 3.250x4.375 in. engine, the tractor produced 20.0 hp at the drawbar and 28.2 hp on the pulley. This Continental was a popular industrial engine of the period. The tractor weighed 4,955 lb., and was fitted with a four-speed transmission, which not only topped out at nearly 20 mph, but also ran through the pulley and offered four belt speeds plus reverse.

Graham brothers used Dodge brothers parts, including Dodge truck brakes.

The tractor's appearance reflected the automotive styling of the day. The tractor had a swept-back streamline look. Ironically, the Graham automobiles leaned in the opposite direction, appearing swept forward as though rushing to meet the wind.

The tractor sales agreement with Sears was an exclusive arrangement that offered the tractor as Graham's only full-size machine. This meant it was available only through Sears' catalogs and retail outlets. The Graham sedans were offered through some of the retail outlets as well.

The relationship for Graham-Paige and Sears ended when Graham-Paige suspended production during World War II. Afterwards, Graham-Paige's president, Joseph Frazer, merged the company with Henry J. Kaiser. Some plans for new tractors were discussed, but instead the company produced two new automobiles, the Kaiser and the Frazer.

Bibliography

This is a listing of some of the main texts consulted. Many more contemporary sources were also used.

Allis-Chalmers, C. H. Wendel, Crestline 1988.

American Farm Tractors, C. H. Wendel, Crestline, 1988.

The Black Book, Phillip Rose, General Motors, n.d.

The Caterpillar Story, Caterpillar, 1990.

The Century of the Reaper, Cyrus McCormick III, Houghton Mifflin, 1931.

Farm Equipment Retailer's Handbook, Arch Merrifield, Farm Equipment Retailing, 1953.

Farm Power: International Harvester, ASAE, 1915, reprint.

Field Boss: Progress in Tractor Power Since 1898, G. R. Gregg, White-New Idea, n.d.

Ford Tractors, Robert Pripps and Andrew Morland, Motorbooks International, 1990.

The Model T Ford Car and Ford Farm Tractor, Victor Page, Norman Henley, 1918.

John Deere: He Gave the World the Steel Plow, Neil M. Clark, private printing, 1937.

John Deere's Company, Wayne Broehl, Doubleday, 1981.

Machines of Plenty, Stewart Holbrook, MacMillan, 1955.

Minneapolis-Moline Tractors 1870–1969, C. H. Wendel and Andrew Morland, Motorbooks International, 1990.

The Modern Gas Tractor: Its Construction, Operation, Application and Repair, Victor Page, Norman Henley, 1913.

My Forty Years With Ford, Charles Sorensen, Norton, 1956.

My Life and Work, Henry Ford, Garden City, 1926.

The Operation, Care and Repair of Farm Machinery, John Deere, 1929.

Nebraska Tractor Tests Since 1920, C. H. Wendel, Crestline, 1985.

Pioneers in Industry: Fairbanks, Morse, Fairbanks, Morse, 1945.

Power Farming With Greater Profit, John Deere, 1937, reprint.

The Science of Successful Threshing, Dingee MacGregor, Robinson, Case, 1899.

The Story of John Deere, Darragh Aldrich, private printing, 1942.

The Traction Engine, James Maggard, David McKay, 1898.

The Why and Wherefore of the Diesel Engine, International Harvester, n.d.

Index